Mail and Mystery, Family and Friends:

DRAMA CURRICULUM FOR SECOND AND THIRD GRADES

by Pamela Gerke and Helen Landalf

YOUNG ACTORS SERIES

SK
A Smith and Kraus Book

A Smith and Kraus Book
Published by Smith and Kraus, Inc.
PO Box 127, Lyme, NH 03768

First Edition: April 1999
10 9 8 7 6 5 4 3 2 1

Cover and Book Design by Julia Hill Gignoux, Freedom Hill Design

The Library of Congress Cataloging-In-Publication Data
Gerke, Pamela.
Mail and mystery, family and friends: drama curriculum for second and
third grades / by Pamela Gerke and Helen Landalf. —1st ed.
p.   cm.   — (Young actors series)
Discography: p.
Includes bibliographical references.
ISBN 1-57525-188-4
1. Drama in education. 2. Drama study and teaching (primary)
I. Title. II. Series: Young actor series.
PN3171.G37   1999
372.66'043—dc21   99-25288
CIP

ACKNOWLEDGMENTS

We would like to acknowledge the following drama specialists who shared their work and philosophies with us: Susan Anderson, Kathleen Edwards, Don Fleming, Jillian Jorgenson, Stacia Keogh, Barbara Lachman, Michelle Landergott, Dr. Barbara McKean, David Miller, Sam Sebesta, and Ted Sod.

We would also like to thank Eileen Aagaard and her third-grade class at Syre Elementary in Shoreline Washington for trying out some of these lessons. Thank you to Dr. Barbara McKean for reviewing our introductory chapters. Thank you to Vi Hilbert for granting us permission to use the story *Da-Hoos-Wheé-Whee,* and for sharing her knowledge of Lushootseed Salish culture. Thank you to Clayton Miller for sharing his knowledge of Dalcroze Eurhythmics. Special thanks to Susan Anderson for her extensive help in mentoring us in role drama work and reviewing our writing.

We would like to thank authors Norah Morgan and Juliana Saxton for their excellent book *Teaching Drama,* and Betty Jane Wagner for her inspiring book *Dorothy Heathcote: Drama as a Learning Medium*, both of which were highly influential in the conception of this curriculum.

Thank you to our book designer Julia Hill Gignoux, and to Marisa Smith, Eric Kraus, and the staff at Smith and Kraus, Inc. for their help and support in creating this book.

*This book is dedicated to Dorothy Heathcote,
the inspiration behind our work, and to all teachers of children
who give so generously of their time, energy, and caring.*

Contents

CHAPTER THREE: HOW TO USE THIS CURRICULUM

CHAPTER FOUR: MANAGING DRAMA ACTIVITIES IN THE CLASSROOM

CHAPTER FIVE: CONNECTING DRAMA TO OTHER SUBJECT AREAS

CHAPTER SIX: STARTING OUT: CREATING A CONTEXT

PART II: EXPLORATION AND RESEARCH ON POSTAL WORKERS

LESSON 1: THE POSTAL WORKERS' TRAINING SCHOOL

LESSON 2: AT THE POST OFFICE

PART III: THE MYSTERY LETTER

PART IV: INTERPRETING, RECORDING, AND PRESENTING THE DESIGNERS' EXPERIENCE

PART V: NEW PERSPECTIVES

PART VI: DRAMA AND LITERATURE

PART VII: PLAY PRODUCTION

THE SCRIPT

Introduction

BY HELEN LANDALF

When I was a young girl, I once spent several weeks constantly peering from under my right hand, as if I were shading my eyes from the sun. Concerned, my teacher asked me if my eyes were bothering me. "No," I replied, "I'm Jack looking down from the bean stalk."

During another period I was convinced that I was Dorothy in *The Wizard of Oz,* and I stopped at every street corner to sing "Somewhere Over the Rainbow."

The ease with which I could slip from one imaginary character or situation to another was almost magical. It felt completely logical to believe that the tree in our backyard was a rocket ship, or that there was a monster under the bed. As an adult, I see the same ability and desire to create an imaginary world in almost every child I come into contact with. Dramatic play is both natural and fundamental to child development, so as a teacher I find that using a child's inborn urge to imagine and play out fantasies is the most effective way to motivate and engage them in learning.

The skills of imagining and expressing seemed so simple and natural — until I was asked, along with my co-author Pamela Gerke, to write this drama curriculum for elementary teachers. Suddenly, I became almost overwhelmed with the complexity of choices that needed to be made about how to present drama to children in a way that would preserve their innate desire to imagine, yet would encourage them to strive for ever higher levels of personal and artistic excellence.

One of the first and most difficult decisions that Pamela and I needed to make was whether we would approach drama education from a performance orientation — giving children the skills necessary for the performance of scenes and plays — or a creative dramatics orientation that was as much concerned with the development of the whole child as with specific drama skills. Although some drama educators believe quite dogmatically that only one of these approaches to children's drama is the "correct" one, Pamela and I share the view that both approaches are important and valid. What was imperative, we both felt, was to present each approach with a focus on the students' process rather than on an audience-oriented product. Our quest became to create a curriculum that would integrate both creative dramatics and theater, yet keep the focus throughout squarely on the creative experience and personal development of the child.

The answer to our dilemma came with our introduction to the work of British drama educator Dorothy Heathcote. Through reading about her methods, talking with teachers who have studied with her and used her approach, and seeing her in action on film, we came to realize that her way of teaching drama was broad enough and deep enough to contain all of the goals we wished to cover in our curriculum. The study of her philosophy led us to the idea of creating an imaginary context or framework within which we could present a multitude of drama experiences.

We hope that using *Mail and Mystery, Families and Friends: Drama Curriculum for Second and Third Grade* will be a unique and enjoyable experience for you and your students. We intend this curriculum to serve as a *method* for implementing drama education in elementary classrooms — one that you can follow page by page throughout the year — as well as a *model* that you can use to create drama lessons of your own, based on this example of a contextually based drama curriculum. Feel free to use the curriculum exactly as we have written it or use it as a starting point for making drama a learning medium for other subject areas as well.

In closing, Pamela and I would like to express the gratitude and admiration that we feel for all who enter the vital profession of being teachers of our children. There is certainly no career as challenging — or as rewarding — and certainly none that makes a greater impact on the future of our world.

PART I
DRAMA IN THE CLASSROOM

Chapter One
WHY DRAMA IN THE CLASSROOM?

From Creative Dramatics to Theater: A Continuum of Learning

The second-graders tiptoe into their classroom. "Shhh...," says their teacher. "We don't want to disturb the animals of the rain forest." "Look!" yells Bobby, pointing toward the coat closet. "Cobra! Ahhh!!!" He pantomimes being choked by a giant snake. The class, used to Bobby's antics, ignores him.

Marian looks down at the floor and freezes. "Jaguar tracks!" she hisses, pointing to the old stains on the carpet in the reading corner. The rest of the class comes over and stares at the stains. "Can you tell how big the jaguar is by its paw prints?" asks the teacher. "Giant!" cries one child. "It's coming to get me!" screams Bobby, who dives under a desk, followed by three other students.

"Don't be silly," Marian says, in her practical tone. "It's obviously a baby." "What do you think, Kyle?" asks the teacher, turning toward the quiet boy at the edge of the group around the carpet stains. Kyle smiles shyly, gets a ruler out of his desk and starts measuring the stains. Several other students run and grab their rulers and excitedly start measuring all the stains on the classroom carpet.

"We need to make a decision," says the teacher. "Should we stay here and try to learn more about the cat that made these tracks or should we continue on to our camp? Remember, we only have two hours until nightfall."

Across the hall in Room 6, the students of Kindergarten 1B rehearse their play. "Places for Scene One!" calls their teacher and everyone scurries to their places for the beginning of *The Adventures of Anansi*. One student wanders around, unsure where to go until her teacher reminds her that The Villagers stand next to the blackboard.

Tasha begins to read: "'How Anansi Got A Thin Waist.' Long ago in West Africa, Anansi the Spider did not look like he does today." "Excuse me, Tasha," says the teacher. "You'll have to speak much louder so that the audience can hear you. Continue, please."

Tasha reads with a tiny bit more volume: "Back then he was big all over and his waistline was very fat." Max enters the classroom from the hallway, with two pillows tied around his waist with a piece of rope. The other students, at various stations around the room, begin to giggle. The teacher chuckles, "Anansi is a pretty funny character." "He's the Trickster!" cries Sara, remembering what her teacher has said about this classic folklore figure. "Yes," says the teacher. "Now who can tell us why it's not okay to laugh and talk from backstage during the performance?"

One student calls out, "Because then the audience can't hear the play!" Another adds, "And they won't pay attention!" "That's right," says the teacher. "Now, let's continue."

In the two scenarios above, both classes are engaged in drama education in the classroom. The first example, where students are improvising an imaginary journey through the rain forest, is of a type of drama called *creative dramatics*. Creative dramatics is a general term referring to a type of activity in which participants create scenes or stories with improvised dialogue and action. It is a "process-centered form of theatre in which participants are guided by a leader to imagine, enact, and reflect upon human experiences" (The Childrens Theatre Association of America). Although creative dramatics can be presented to others, usually in the form of a demonstration, its goal is the personal development of the participants rather than the satisfaction of an audience.

The second example is of a class engaged in the art of *theater*: preparing a performance in which a script is used and in which the purpose is to communicate the story effectively to an audience. In a theater experience, performers gain skills related to communicating their artistic work to others and are able to evaluate the effects of their words and actions; however, the satisfaction of the audience is the goal. To put it simply, creative dramatics is for *the participant* and theater is for *the audience*.

Below is a visual image of the spectrum of drama activities possible with second- and third-graders (thanks to Dr. Barbara McKean). Although we have sequenced the lessons in this curriculum as (roughly) progressing from the left to the right on this spectrum, any or all of these activities can be used at any time with second- and third-grade students. None of the activities on this spectrum are more important for children's development than any of the others: Children can benefit as much from performing in scripted play productions as they can from participating in creative play activities. The key to being an effective teacher of drama is in identifying which of the activities on this spectrum best suits your own personal teaching style and effectively addresses the needs of your students.

(Also see "Understanding Dramatic Art" in the introductory section to the play script in Part VII for more about the structure and elements of theater and about the "meaning frame" and "expressive frame," as defined by Morgan and Saxton in *Teaching Drama*.)

"Meaning Frame"– – – – – – – – – – – – – – – *"Expressive Frame"*

creative play	**story drama**	**scenes**
free make-believe	*improvise a known story*	*work with a script*

creative dramatics	**improvisation**	**theater**
structured activities, including simple improvisations	*more complex scenes; role drama*	*performance: play or other script*

Developing Skills in a Dramatic Context

Mail and Mystery, Families and Friends covers the entire spectrum above, as appropriate for second- and third-grade students. This drama curriculum has at its core a technique called *role drama,* also known as *contextual drama.* This is an umbrella strategy that lays out an overall context for exploring curricular subjects via drama. The curricular subject explored in this book is, in fact, drama itself; however, role dramas can be used to pique students' interest and motivate exploration in other academic areas as well (see Chapter 5, "Connecting Drama to Other Subject Areas" and other suggestions for integrating drama with other subjects in the "Variations" for each lesson).

Within the context presented in this book, students explore a variety of drama strategies including: games, exercises, movement activities, pantomime, and dramatic play, as well as the sharing of their skills and the results of their drama lessons in public presentations. In the final sections of this curriculum, we extend the dramatic context over a range of activities centering on the interpretation and dramatization of literature and the performance of a scripted play.

Dorothy Heathcote, one of the pioneers of role drama (known as "educational drama" in Great Britain and Canada) refers to this type of drama experience as "a conscious employment of the elements of drama to educate—to literally bring out what children already know but don't yet know they know." (Betty Jane Wagner, *Dorothy Heathcote: Drama as a Learning Medium*).

The theme of *Mail and Mystery, Families and Friends* is family and community. The context of this curriculum supposes that students are a group of stamp and sticker designers who enter a competition to design a new postage stamp series that honors Postal Workers (the Postal System being a service that unites the community). Through lessons that develop drama skills, students engage in a variety of Post Office–related activites as "research" for their stamp designs. At one point, the Designers become temporary Postal Detectives and work on solving the case of a certain "Mystery Letter." This Letter engages students in creating a role drama about two family members who have become separated and who are reunited via the efforts of the Postal Detectives. Students then recreate their Mystery Letter drama as the basis for their postage stamp designs, depicted in a series of narrated tableaux, and present their designs in a Public Sharing Event.

Students then further explore the theme of family and community in a variety of drama activities, including dramatic interpretations of children's literature and preparation of a play performance of a Native American (Lushootseed Salish) story in which family and community roles are prominent. Teachers are encouraged to extend this dramatic context to other areas of the curriculum, including: community studies (touring your local post office), math (sorting, counting, and classifying stamps or letters), science (paper making), art (paper making; designing stamps), literature (stories of families or communities), and social studies (the history and culture of the Lushootseed Salish people of Western Washington; the history and culture of the country from which the Mystery Letter comes).

Educational and Developmental Benefits of Drama

One of the fundamental ways in which children relate to themselves and their environment is to make believe. Because imaginative play is a key factor in brain and body development in children, drama education is a valuable avenue for facilitating children's growth. Educational jargon aside, drama is a powerful teaching tool because, quite simply, it's fun for children. Drama offers a great potential for learning for it engages students' interest and curiosity, holds their attention, and serves as a powerful motivator for children to ask questions and explore new terrain.

As an art form, drama is intrinsically worthy of inclusion in the education of children for it teaches expressive use of body and language, helps develop skills in collaboration and communication. As in language arts, drama is concerned with understanding human experience and creating symbols to represent inner meaning. Drama education teaches children (and adults for that matter) to think like an actor thinks. An actor must think deeply about his character and intentions, understand the themes and symbolism of the dramatic work being explored, be self-disciplined and show perserverance with regard to the study and rehearsal of the work—including time lines and memorization—be concerned with communicating expressively and effectively, and work well with others.

Drama can also be employed as a learning medium to explore other subjects besides the art of drama. Drama activities can bring subject matter to life, stimulating children's curiosity and motivation to learn and providing a means for children to relate the material being presented to their own, personal experiences. ArtsConnection, an arts-in-education organization in New York City, is based on the belief that teachers who use the arts in their day-to-day classroom work "discover an ally in the arts: a disciplined way of knowing and learning that is both lively and focused, that can reveal and inspire, and that connects students to their education in a meaningful way." ("Adapting Arts Processes to the Classroom," abstract).

Drama and the Multiple Intelligences

Howard Gardner, a developmental psychologist and neuropsychologist, defines intelligence as "an ability to solve a problem or to make something that's valued in at least one culture or community." In his influential book *Frames of Mind*, Gardner identifies seven intelligences: linguistic, musical, logical-mathematical, spatial, bodily kinesthetic, intrapersonal, and interpersonal. The lessons in this drama curriculum, covering the full spectrum of drama activities from creative dramatics to theater, engage all of these intelligences (with the exception of logical-mathematical, which is touched upon only peripherally).

Gardner has also added another "half" of an intelligence that he calls "existential," the ability to deal with fundamental questions about existence, such as: Who are we? Where do we come from? The arts in general speak to this intelligence also, for they encourage curiosity and awareness of matters that are not scientifically quantifiable but that are concepts humanity has been pondering for eons.

In the following list of Skills Developed Through Drama Education, and throughout this entire book, we lay out the educational and developmental foundation for our curriculum. In addition, we want to mention here that another fundamental reason to include drama in the classroom is, quite simply, that it's good for children. The arts make us whole, healthy, and happy and connect us with the "left hand of knowing"—that unnamable source of wisdom. The arts feed our souls...and this is reason enough to include them in all of our lives.

Skills Developed Through Drama Education

The skills of benefit to children's education and development that are covered in this curriculum are in five general areas:

- Physical Development / Kinesthetic Skills
- Artistic Development / Drama and Theater Skills
- Mental Development / Thinking Skills
- Personal Development / Intrapersonal Skills
- Social Development / Interpersonal Skills

Many skills in each area overlap into the other areas. That drama activities contribute to all of these crucial areas of child development is precisely why drama is ideal for children's education. These skills should be seen as areas of potential, continual development, not as finite, quantifiable goals.

Physical Development / Kinesthetic Skills:

Use of the senses

Use of the whole body in movement

Awareness and control of body parts

Awareness and control of the body in space

Artistic Development / Drama and Theater Skills:

Expressive use of body and movement

Expressive use of voice and language

Commitment to believing in imaginary situations

Understanding and expression of character

Understanding and expression of setting (includes time, place, and situation)

Use and study of dramatic form

Story creation / playwriting

Communication with an audience

Development of discriminating perception as an audience member

Artistic collaboration (see Interpersonal Skills)

Mental Development / Thinking Skills:

Use and development of imagination and creativity

Ability to focus attention

Use and development of powers of observation and awareness of details

Use and development of flexible thinking and spontaneity

Use and development of memory

Use and development of problem-solving skills

Ability to sequence time and events

Organization and synthesis of ideas

Ability to understand and use symbols and metaphors

Personal Development / Intrapersonal Skills:

Awareness and expression of inner thoughts, feelings, and values

Development of self-esteem and confidence

Ability to assess and improve one's own work

Perseverance in a task

Development of resiliency and hope (by imagining "what can be" versus "what is")

Development of a sense of self-determination, the belief that one has the power to affect one's own destiny

Embodiment of story, myth, and archetype

Appreciation and enjoyment of the arts

Social Development / Interpersonal Skills:

Ability to follow directions

Communication (both listening and speaking)

Development of trust in and empathy for others

Collaboration and negotiation with others

Ability to give and receive constructive feedback

Public presentation: the outward expression of inner thoughts and feelings

Development of appropriate behavior as an audience member

Chapter Two
THE CLASSROOM TEACHER
AS DRAMA INSTRUCTOR

Arts in Education

That the arts play an important part in the education of children is an idea that is becoming more and more accepted in society and implemented by educational systems. Supported by numerous studies that prove that the arts aid in the physical, cognitive, social, and emotional development of children, increasing numbers of state education departments and local school districts in the United States are mandating the inclusion of the arts in their core curricula and are adopting standards for the performing and visual arts.

For the typical classroom teacher, these mandates may appear daunting. With good reason, classroom teachers may feel unqualified to teach the arts without proper training and experience. This drama curriculum is designed with the classroom teacher in mind. It is not, however, intended to replace drama specialists and artists-in-residence in schools. Professionals such as these are much needed in children's education and can never be simply replaced with a book such as this one. Yet, with proper preparation and support, elementary school classroom teachers can prove capable of teaching some of the basics of drama, as well as using drama as an entry point into other areas of the curriculum.

Support for the Teacher as Drama Instructor

Hopefully, the classroom teacher who teaches drama will have the full support of the school administration and faculty, both as fellow proponents of arts in education and in practical matters, such as ensuring that teachers have adequate space and time periods for drama activities. In addition, support by students' parents and their active participation in classroom drama activities will greatly add to the success of a drama program. Children whose parents are engaged and active in their child's learning process typically have better academic success than otherwise, and parental involvement helps to build advocacy for quality arts education in the community. We recommend that classroom teachers ask parents to get involved in drama lessons as volunteers, guest characters "in role," and audience members.

Whenever possible, classroom teachers can and should advocate for the inclusion of arts professionals in residencies at their schools. Teachers can learn best from professional artists who teach by example, lead teacher-in-service trainings, and offer other guidance and support that only someone who works in this field can provide. Investigate the funding and other support systems for bringing artists-in-residence into your school. Initiate projects with working artists—many artists are eager to share their expertise with children, given the opportunity.

Attitudes and Values

The essential principles of good drama pedagogy are the same as for teaching in general: respect for the ideas, feelings, processes, creativity, and originality of all students, and belief in the potential of all individuals to learn and grow. A classroom teacher who chooses to include drama in the curriculum must also be committed to the value of arts in education and be willing to embrace the process of creating art.

The artistic process is a continually evolving experience of experimenting and being open to inspiration. What distinguishes the arts from some of the other areas of the core curriculum is that in art there is no right and wrong, such as: "The sky can only be painted blue." In teaching the arts, there are often no quantifiable, verifiable, "right" answers. Like all good teachers, a drama instructor does not expect students to give answers that the instructor wants to hear, but rather is primarily interested in sparking students' interest and curiosity and facilitating their processes of self-discovery and creativity (also see "Asking Questions," below).

Children's drama teachers need to remain focused on the *process* of the drama activities rather than the finished *product* and should not put pressure on children to perform for the public as skilled actors. The skill level needed to perform effectively and expressively takes a lot of time and effort to develop, and it is unfair to children to expect them to achieve this level of competence in verbal and physical communication before they are ready. Building skill in communicating is, however, an important task in child development and we therefore include several opportunities in this curriculum for students to share their work with an audience. Nevertheless, the goal of children's drama education is to provide experiences that lead to the physical, mental, emotional, and social development of the child, not the achievement of a high level of professional performance skill.

In order to keep the focus of drama lessons on the educational process of students rather than on creating a final product, a drama instructor needs to respect the originality of all students and to trust them to find their own ways to express ideas and feelings. The nature of improvisation and much else in the art of drama is about trusting oneself to create spontaneously. The best drama instructors are those who establish an atmosphere in which it is safe to take risks and in which spontaneous responses are celebrated. The teacher who is supportive and positive about the contributions of all students thereby assures everyone that it is safe to "go out on a limb" creatively.

A safe climate is also created by drama teachers who engage students in decision making and creative planning, and who model constructive, positive feedback and self-evaluation. Artists must regularly evaluate their work. Drama education provides an excellent means for students to learn the self-regulating skills of assessing one's own work and learning processes, as well as discovering how to be a discriminating observer of the work of others and how to give helpful, critical feedback.

Above all, a classroom teacher who teaches drama must maintain a positive attitude, a healthy sense of humor, and a willingness to be flexible. The unexpected often happens in drama activities and teachers need to be willing to "go with the flow" and allow an activity to move in an entirely new, unplanned direction when inspiration strikes. A teacher who is flexible in this way truly respects the artistic process and the originality of all students. And don't forget to have some fun along the way—doing drama activities with kids is truly one of life's most joyful experiences!

Expectations, Goals, and Assessment

Teachers can and should expect their students to participate in drama activities under the same high standards they uphold for all classroom work: to come prepared, stay focused, listen and respond appropriately, contribute ideas to the group, take creative risks, and get along with others. These criteria are no different than those expected of professional artists. Artists must be self-disciplined in order to succeed. Drama education teaches the skills of self-regulation that students can then apply to other academic areas.

The first chapter, "Why Drama in the Classroom?" includes a list of the educational and developmental skills developed through drama education. This list can be used by teachers as a guide for determining educational goals for drama lessons. It can also be used to assess the progress of individual students with the objective of furthering each individual's continuing development in these areas. This list should not, however, be used as an evaluation checklist against which students are graded. Response to art is subjective and artistic achievement is not measurable in the same way that achievement in other areas can be measured. The skills we have outlined should be seen as areas of focus in the continuing education of children, not as end points of perfection.

In order to record the progress of students while using this drama curriculum, make one photocopy of the "Skills Developed through Drama Education" (Chapter 1) for each student. Write your observations of each student's progress on their sheet as a written narrative, rather than as a quantifiable evaluation.

Creating a Context: The Teacher In Role

As we mentioned in Chapter 1, this curriculum is centered around a type of drama called role drama, which establishes an overall context that connects all of the lessons. One of the most powerful methods for teaching within a role drama is the "teacher in role." In this method, the teacher participates in the drama while still monitoring the learning experiences of students. The teacher in role can effectively manage the group, guide students in making decisions about their drama, establish mood, help deepen students' belief in the drama, move students toward the teacher's educational objectives, and facilitate students' self-reflection on their experiences within the drama.

In order to determine what role to represent in a drama, teachers must clarify their goals for their students and assess the social health of their class. The role a teacher selects is determined by the point of view that will best forward the teacher's educational objectives. Each type of role offers different opportunities for facilitating the drama or managing the group. The following are classifications and examples of the kinds of roles a teacher might choose in a classroom role drama. (See *Teaching Drama* by Norah Morgan and Juliana Saxton for more in-depth analysis of teacher in role.)

AUTHORITY: For a class that is diffuse and unable to self-regulate, or for students who are new to drama and are as yet unable to take responsibility for their own drama, a teacher might choose to take a role of authority, for example: the Professor, the Queen, or the Chief Surgeon. The role of a person with authority puts the teacher in a position of leadership, of being the "one who knows," the one who can disseminate useful information and manipulate the group as needed. In a role of authority, the teacher has high status, akin to the traditional instructive mode. (Note: "Status" here refers to the teacher's position of power in relation to her students and carries with it obvious implications for managing the class.)

HELPLESS: When a teacher wants to bring his students together in a common cause, he might choose a helpless role, such as an Injured or Lost Person, or a person who is needing explanation or direction. A helpless role creates the need for students to approach the teacher with compassion and guidance, and it is a very effective role for uniting students who may otherwise be divisive. The helpless role carries a low status for the teacher while it gives students a relatively high status, thereby engendering students' assumption of responsibility.

FACILITATOR: A facilitator role can be taken with a class of students who are self-sufficient and able to seek their own information while the teacher moves among them, offering suggestions and resources when requested. Typical facilitator roles include: an authority outside of the central action, for example the Chamberlain who is available as an advisor to the court; or a fringe role, such as someone who is a part of the scene and can ask questions about it, but who is neither a member of the group nor an authority figure. Examples of fringe roles might be: a Hospital Receptionist or TV Reporter. A facilitator role generally carries a middle status, for in this role a teacher can extend or withdraw responsibility or authority from the students as she deems appropriate.

MEMBER OF THE GROUP: For a class with good social health, a teacher might choose to act as a member of the group in which students are in role, learning and making decisions alongside them. As a member, a teacher can take several possible roles. A high status role would be that of a leader who has the group's best interests in mind, such as Chief Scout or Head Archeologist. Another possible member role that is particularly useful is that of "second-in-command." This role, which carries a high to middle status, gives the teacher some authority to manipulate the drama but, unlike the first-in-command, places the teacher on a more equal footing with the group. Examples of second-in-command roles are: First Mate or Vice President. As a member of the group, the teacher can also take a role that is on the fringe of the group yet still allows the teacher to observe, comment, or participate in some way, such as: the Mascot or the Court Stenographer. A role as fringe member of the group carries a middle to low status.

Facilitating Reflection

The drama instructor in the classroom is ideally poised to help students see below the surface of actions to their deeper meaning. Through the imaginative element of drama, students' subjective feelings, experiences, and accumulated knowledge come into play. This invocation of the subjective, inner world is one of the most exciting aspects of drama in the classroom because it provides a medium that leads students to discover that they have something in common with the universal human experience and, therefore, with all that has gone before.

The teacher who is aware of this linkage between subjective feeling and dramatic form takes the opportunity, whenever possible, to lead students to reflect on the meaning of any particular moment in their drama activities. Guiding students to deepen in their understanding of their own experiences, "to find the feel of what they know," (in Dorothy Heathcote's words) brings them to greater self-awareness. It also awakens them to discover the joy of learning and the desire to know more.

In education, making the connection between one's own personal experiences and external informational material, such as books, is referred to as "cracking the code"; that is, students no longer feel separate from the material and find that learning is exciting and fun. The ability of drama to serve both as a conduit for finding universal meaning and to "crack the code" of education makes it a powerful entry into all curricular subjects. Teachers also have the opportunity to facilitate students' reflection on the broader issues of the subject of the role drama itself. For example, a drama about a visit to the zoo might engender reflection about endangered species of animals; or a drama about a family reunion might stimulate reflection about the definition of "family."

Asking Questions

In teaching drama, as in all teaching, the ability to articulate thought-provoking questions and to respond sensitively to the answers given is one of the most useful skills a teacher can develop. All teachers should prioritize developing and practicing the skill of asking questions that encourage learning and growth.

Questions asked by a teacher can be either limiting or freeing for students. Limiting questions are those in which the teacher conveys, either subtley or overtly, his own expectation of the "right" answer, that the student then tries to discover and deliver. In this case, question asking does not support the healthy development of children, except perhaps by honing their ability to satisfy an external authority and avoid conflict. Freeing questions, on the other hand, are those that signal to the student that one particular answer is neither expected nor desired. The teacher does not pose the question in the status of higher authority but instead invites the student to participate as an equal in the discussion, thus freeing the student to answer honestly and without fear of retribution.

Freeing questions encourage students to develop the habit of looking at something from many perspectives because the teacher has established the concept that knowledge is not finite. Freeing questions are asked honestly, with true interest in the response, not with the implication that the teacher already knows the answer and is only seeking to find out if the student knows it as well. Statements that evoke a response can also be freeing if they are open-ended, such as statements beginning with "I wonder..." or, "I can't imagine why..." or, "You know, it seems to me...."

Teachers should be aware of their purpose in asking a particular question. Questions can be used by teachers to establish a dramatic mood, motivate a group decision, encourage shy students to contribute, stimulate students to research, or encourage insight into the significance of a dramatic experience. Asking questions can also be used by teachers to manage the class or discover information about students, such as by seeking to discover what they do or don't know or understand, or clarifying what students think or how they feel about their knowledge. A teacher's questions should be motivated by her educational goals for students. Well-selected questions can stimulate students to interpret their experiences, identify what is significant for them in those experiences, consider alternatives, make suppositions, or discover their personal feelings or values.

Equally important as articulating appropriate questions is the matter of how the question is posed. The teacher should be aware of word choice, tone of voice, and body language so as to not imply any expectation of a particular response. Also important is how the teacher responds to the answer given. In drama, teachers must listen respectfully to all suggestions and statements made by students, while encouraging them to consider the implications of each possibility. Teachers can point out the probable results of a specific action, thus leading students to consider the consequences of their ideas before making final decisions. When students do make a decision about their drama, the teacher must be willing to go along with their choices (as long as they do not violate the teacher's own limits for appropriate behavior). In honoring students' decisions, the teacher helps them feel a sense of ownership of the drama activity, thereby leading to greater enthusiasm and participation than if students feel they have no say in the decision-making process.

The following types of questions should be avoided: those that elicit a yes/no response and, in certain situations, those beginning with "Why?" and "How did/do you feel?" Yes/no responses don't require any real depth of thought. The question, "Why?" should be avoided with regard to personal responses. Often students don't know why they feel a certain way or why they made certain decisions (do you?) and they may feel defensive when asked to explain. Your questions should focus on the context and essence of the experience and you should ask "Why?" only when trying to obtain factual information.

The question, "How did/do you feel?" should also be avoided as it can engender vague responses or lead students to feel that you are prying into their personal feelings. Dorothy Heathcote recommends that teachers ask questions directed at the students' *concerns,* rather than asking students what their feelings are (Morgan and Saxton, *Teaching Drama*). For example, "What were you concerned about when you discovered that the Queen was missing?" Or, "What were your concerns when the pirates came on board?"

How to Prepare to Teach Drama

One of the best ways to prepare for doing drama activities in the classroom is to take an active interest in your own artistic development. For example, take a drama class, participate in a community performance, go to see theater performances, read plays and books about drama. Studying and participating in any other art form besides drama, especially performing arts such as music or dance, will help you to appreciate the artistic process. In other words: DO IT!

Read books and magazines dedicated to the art of teaching drama, a number of which are listed in the Bibliography, and otherwise prepare yourself by learning about the philosophy and methods of teaching creative processes. Join a local or national organization for the advancement of children's drama education. For additional support and ideas talk with other teachers who do drama activities or have worked with theater artists in their classroom.

Conclusion

This chapter briefly outlines what we believe are the key points for assuming the mantle of teaching drama in the classroom. For more information about teaching drama, see the Commentary at the end of each lesson, as well as the Glossary for definitions of drama terms. We agree with Dorothy Heathcote who says that "the time has come to show all teachers, including classroom teachers, how they can use drama to achieve something that cannot be attained as effectively in any other way" (Betty Jane Wagner, *Dorothy Heathcote Drama As A Learning Medium*). Drama is indeed a mighty force for children's education when it is used to aid in the development of the whole child, to evoke understanding and a feeling of connection to the universal human experience, to enhance creativity and aesthetics, and to stimulate curiosity, enthusiasm for learning, and joy.

Chapter Three

HOW TO USE THIS CURRICULUM

If you are like many classroom teachers, the lessons in this book may be very different from the types of activities you usually engage in with your students. Or, if you are lucky enough to be working in a school or district where teachers are supported in integrating the arts into the curriculum, this type of material may be more familiar to you. In either case this chapter will help guide you in determining how this Drama Curriculum can fit into your classroom schedule, acquaint you with how the material in the curriculum is organized, and assist you in effectively presenting the lessons in this book.

How the Drama Curriculum is Organized

Mail and Mystery, Families and Friends: Drama Curriculum for Second and Third Grade is organized around a specific imaginary context. The context supposes that the students are members of a Stamp and Sticker Design Company who enter a contest to design postage stamps with the theme "Honoring U.S. Postal Workers." This imaginary framework underlies every lesson and activity in the curriculum and acts as a motivation for students to learn and practice drama skills. Because the context is so important to the presentation of the curriculum, teachers are urged to read the entire book before beginning instruction, paying particular attention to the chapter "Starting Out: Creating a Context."

The context created for the *Drama Curriculum* need not be isolated to the periods set aside for drama activities. The second- and third-grade drama curriculum context provides a perfect opportunity for the teacher to extend the study of the U.S. mail system and family and community life to other areas of the academic curriculum throughout the year. Both the drama curriculum and your academic curriculum will be enriched by relating them to this context.

Mail and Mystery, Families and Friends is divided into six sections that move from creative drama (experiencing) to formal drama (presenting), from generation (creating a story) to interpretation (putting on a play from a script), and from simple to complex dramatic skills. The order of the sections of this curriculum is based on these progressions and, for this reason, we suggest you do the lessons in the order presented in this book. In saying this, we do not mean to suggest that creative drama is merely a prerequisite for formal drama, or that putting on a play is the end goal to be attained in a drama program. Each section of this curriculum contains valuable learning experiences for students, and no part of the curriculum is to be considered a means to an end. You may choose to present the sections of this curriculum in a different order, such as beginning with a production of the play, *Da-Hoos-Wheé-Whee* and ending the year's drama study with the spontaneous role drama "The Mystery Letter." However, we believe the best results for your students will be attained by using the sequence we have prescribed.

Each section of the second- and third-grade drama curriculum is divided into individual lessons, lasting fifteen to fifty minutes each. Most lessons contain one to three related activities. You may do all of a lesson's activities during a single drama session, or do just one or two and save the remaining activities for another day, depending on the amount of time you have. You may also choose to omit one or more activities entirely. Once an activity has been introduced you can repeat it in any subsequent session as a warm up. You are also encouraged to try one or more of the variations listed for each activity.

We suggest that you present a lesson from the second- and third-grade drama curriculum approximately once a week in sessions lasting fifteen to fifty minutes each. Lessons 7, 8, 9, and 10, "The Mystery Letter," should be presented on consecutive days. Preparing an informal presentation of the play *Da-Hoos-Wheé-Whee* will require several rehearsals per week, each lasting 30–45 minutes.

Using the Drama Curriculum Lessons

Once you have familiarized yourself with the organization of the curriculum and have carefully read all the introductory chapters and lessons, you are ready to start teaching the *Drama Curriculum* lessons. Each lesson contains important information under the following headings:

LESSON NUMBER AND TITLE
ACTIVITY TITLES, TIME REQUIRED

The specific activities that make up each lesson, as well as the approximate time required to present each activity, can be found at the top of the lesson's first page. Be aware that presentation times will vary depending on your presentation style and the responses of your students.

CONTEXT

This heading tells you how this particular lesson or activity fits into the overall context of the entire curriculum. The context is written in one or two sentences that you can share with your students before beginning the lesson. Feel free to change the wording of the context statement as you feel appropriate.

SKILLS

This heading lists the major skills from the "List of Skills Developed Through Drama Education," pages 9–11, that are introduced or developed in the course of the activity. Once a skill has been introduced, students will naturally use it in subsequent lessons, even if it is not listed under this heading. For example, if the ability to focus attention is introduced in one activity, it will be practiced in most subsequent activities, even when the major focus of those activities is on introducing new skills.

In addition to the drama skills listed for each activity, you may find that a particular lesson also provides an opportunity for you to focus on an educational goal related to another subject area. For example, you may choose to emphasize curricular material about the U.S. Postal System or family and communities along with the presentation of drama skills in some lessons in Parts I, II, and III of this curriculum.

MATERIALS / PREPARATION

Under this heading are listed any specific materials or preparation steps required or suggested in order to teach the lesson, including set-up of the physical space and construction of props.

MUSICAL SUGGESTIONS

The majority of the lessons in this book can be presented without music. However, music is very motivating for children and can help students feel more involved and less self-conscious. Several lessons in this book suggest specific musical selections, but most of the lessons in which music is required or beneficial can be successfully presented using any selection from the Discography at the end of this book or music from your own collection. In general, New Age, classical, ethnic, or folk music is more conducive to creative response than is currently popular music, and instrumental music is more effective than music with lyrics.

PROCEDURE

The lesson's procedure is written as a step-by-step guide to presenting the lesson. The procedure represents one possible way to conduct the lesson. However, you are welcome and encouraged to adapt the manner of presentation to your teaching style and to the particular needs of your students. The most important thing to remember as you teach the drama lessons in this book is to maintain a flexible, nonjudgmental attitude that allows students a safe forum for freedom of self-expression.

COMMENTARY

The commentary provided at the end of each lesson or activity provides you with additional, pertinent information about how to successfully present the lesson and about the significance of the lesson in the development of dramatic skills, or in child development in general.

VARIATIONS

These are ideas on alternative ways to present the activity or ways to extend the activity to enhance learning in other areas of your curriculum.

LITERATURE SELECTIONS

The lessons in Part VI: Drama and Literature contain the text of any written selections used in the lesson. Alternative literature selections that can be used in a similar way are listed at the end of each of these lessons. All selections mentioned in the literature section and throughout the book can be found in the Bibliography.

Making Space for Drama

It is a sad truth that adequate space for drama and movement activities in the typical elementary school building is minimal. While most schools and school districts spend thousands of dollars on computer equipment, educational planners often do not consider providing adequate movement space for children in order for them to use the natural learning resource of their own bodies and imaginations. Therefore it becomes the responsibility of the classroom teacher to adjust, adapt...and advocate for change in this vital area.

Try the following suggestions to maximize space for drama activities in your classroom:

1. Create a routine for clearing as much space as possible in your classroom. Challenge students to rearrange furniture in record amounts of time (and to put it back when the lesson is over).

2. When classroom furniture must stay in place, use any open space at the front or back of your classroom for drama activities. Many activities can also incorporate students traveling up and down aisles between furniture.

3. Have only half of the class or small groups of students participate in an activity at a time with the rest of the class watching. Repeat the activity again with the other group(s) participating, or rotate giving students a turn to participate on different days.

As an alternative to presenting drama activities in the classroom, use other open spaces in your school building. Try the music room, gym, lunchroom, stage, computer lab, library, and so on. It is also fun to do a drama activity outdoors.

Troubleshooting

Sometimes, despite your best efforts, you may find yourself in the middle of a drama activity that seems "stuck": The students just don't know what to do. In this situation, try the following:

- Give an example or demonstration of the kind of responses that are possible.
- Do only one part of a lesson instead of the entire lesson.
- Take a role in a drama that allows you to give guidance within the context of the story. (For more on this approach, as well as other hints for managing drama activities, see Chapter 4, "Managing Drama Activities in the Classroom.")
- Stop, and try again on another day!

Teacher Self-Assessment

At some point after a lesson is completed you will want to assess the effectiveness of your presentation. We suggest waiting at least an hour or two before making an assessment because by that time you will be able to be more objective and less self-critical.

First, think about what went well in the lesson. When were the students particularly engaged? What were some really creative responses you observed? At what points did you feel that they really "got" the content of the lesson?

Next, take a look at any difficulties or problems you encountered and try to determine their cause. Were your directions to students unclear? Did the students need more direction during the transitions from one part of the lesson to the next? Did you allow a student's negative behavior to garner too much of your attention? Be as specific as you can about the cause of any difficulties to help yourself avoid them in the future.

Last of all, just as you praise your students for striving for their highest potential, treat yourself well—no matter how the lesson went—for doing something that is new and challenging for you. You will find that, over time, leading your students in drama activities seems less overwhelming and will, instead, become vastly rewarding to both you and your students.

For information on assessment of students see the section on "Expectations, Goals, and Assessment" in Chapter 2, "The Classroom Teacher as Drama Instructor."

We hope you and your students will enjoy *Mail and Mystery, Family and Friends: Drama Curriculum for Second and Third Grade.* We encourage you to experiment, take risks, dare to fail... and to succeed. Have fun, and revel in the growth and depth of learning that drama will bring to your classroom.

Chapter Four
MANAGING DRAMA ACTIVITIES
IN THE CLASSROOM

Many teachers, when imagining leading their students in a drama activity, envision a scene of noisy, directionless chaos. Unfortunately, the fear of such an occurrence often prevents these teachers from even attempting to do drama in their classrooms. While a misdirected drama activity can certainly lead to noisy confusion, a well-planned, well-executed lesson leads to engaged, motivated activity.

When students are engaged in drama activities, they are enthusiastic and excited, and they are actively involved with the content of the lesson and with each other. In other words, they're responding exactly the way we, as educators, should want them to respond. However, this type of active learning requires students to move about and speak to one another more than some teachers are comfortable with. The discomfort some teachers feel when faced with noisy, active learning is based on a now outdated cultural standard for student behavior that maintains that students are not learning unless they are sitting quietly at their desks. However, our current understanding of child development and learning styles tells us that the more physically and emotionally a child is involved in learning, the deeper and longer-lasting that learning will be. Thus, we have to change our idea of what learning looks like in order to embrace drama as an appropriate educational activity.

Another aspect of doing drama that may be daunting to some teachers is the fact that, in a drama lesson—particularly in role drama—students take the lead in controlling the direction of the activity. The teacher is present as a guide and facilitator rather than being completely in charge of the outcome of the lesson. This requires teachers, many of whom are accustomed to being at the helm of a learning situation, to let go of their idea of how a drama lesson "should" progress so that their students' creativity can shine through.

Just as we must teach children the rules of a game before they can play it safely and successfully, we must educate them about *how* to engage in drama activities. In most classrooms drama is not part of the usual school day. There is no reason that students in such classrooms would know how to behave during a drama lesson. But often teachers who have never introduced drama before will try it once, then give up altogether because their students did not respond in the way they expected. This is as unfair to students as it would be to give long division problems to a class that had never been introduced to long division, then say "never again" when they failed to solve the problems correctly!

This chapter will give you some general guidelines for leading your students in drama activities. Keep in mind as you read that "Practice makes perfect" and the more you use drama in your classroom the more positively and appropriately your students will respond.

Setting Clear Expectations

As in any teaching situation, it is of vital importance to set clear boundaries and expectations for behavior. It is often helpful to have your students collaborate with you in formulating a set of rules specifically for drama sessions. An example of such a set of rules might be:

Listen and follow directions.
Move carefully, touch gently.
Respect the ideas of others.
Do excellent work.

It is best to state rules in a positive frame—that is, describing what students can and should do—rather than telling students what they should not do. You may also want to set behavioral expectations specific to the space you are working in, such as "Move only on the floor of the gym and stay off the bleachers." The more clear you can be at the outset about what kind of behavior you expect the more safe your students will feel and the more positively they will respond.

It is useful to have a "Freeze" signal: a signal that immediately stops all speaking and activity. A beat on a drum or tambourine works well for this purpose, as does briefly turning off the lights in the classroom. It is a good idea to set up the freeze signal at the beginning of the very first drama lesson, as we have done in Lesson 1 of this curriculum, and to give the students a chance to practice responding to it several times.

Giving Clear Directions

It is very possible for a drama activity to fail because directions were not given clearly. The lessons in this book have been written so as to facilitate your making the directions to students as clear as possible. It is important that students are always told where to go to begin a new activity and what to do when they get there. They need to be told how to engage in the activity and what to do when the activity has been completed. For suggestions on how to give directions in role, see "Managing in Role," below.

The most common place for management to break down is in the transition between two sections of a lesson. For example, if the whole class does an improvisation and the students are then asked to get into partners to work on a movement activity, the transition from working as a whole class to working in partners could be problematic. (For suggestions on how to solve this problem see the section "Organizing Groups," below.) It is important to plan exactly how the transition will take place and to communicate that plan to students.

Managing in Role

There may be many occasions when you will be able to set behavioral expectations and give directions within the context of the specific dramatic activity your students are engaged in. For example, if you wish your students to speak quietly you might, in a dramatic whisper, say "We must speak quietly or the Queen will overhear us!" Or, if you wish students to keep their movements within a certain area of the room you might say, "Remember that the campsite is surrounded by quicksand. One step past this line and you will never be seen again." Setting expectations in this way not only makes clear to students how they should behave, but it also deepens their involvement in the drama situation. Children delight in seeing their teacher play an imaginary role and often respond more willingly than they would if the teacher gave directions in her usual "authority role."

Facilitating Group Decision Making

Creative drama activities, such as those found in this curriculum, often require students to engage in group decision making. There are several ways that you, as a teacher, can facilitate the decision-making process depending upon the amount of time you wish students to spend making a decision, the relative importance of the decision itself, and your overall goal for the activity.

In making a fairly important decision, such as how a drama will begin or end or what type of problem will occur, it may be best to spend the time required for a group to come to consensus. You can help guide this process by making students aware of the implications contained in each suggestion they make. For example, if a student suggests that everyone in the drama be killed, you can point out one of the implications of that choice—that no one will be left to tell the story of what happened. Making students aware of the implications of each possible choice helps them to draw rational conclusions, often resulting in a collective agreement.

In making a less crucial decision, or in a case where a consensus cannot be reached, it is expedient to have students take a majority-rule vote. It's often best to narrow the vote to only two or three possible choices, for example: "Shall we journey by plane or by train?" Be aware that voting can sometimes lead to popularity contests or girls-against-boys battles. We recommend that, when voting, you keep students focused on how the issue under debate relates to the drama rather than allowing it to become a contest between students.

When making a relatively unimportant decision or when the group has come to an impasse, it is sometimes best to simply take the first, workable suggestion offered and move on from there. For example, if you need a name for a person in your drama you can say, "What would be a good name for this person?" If the first student's response is "Max!" and that is an appropriate name, simply say, "Okay, the name of the person is Max." Then continue on without debating the issue further or taking other suggestions.

In all situations where group decision making is required you, as the teacher, must be aware of your goal. If you want the group to feel complete ownership of a particular decision and to practice the valuable process of group collaboration, you may decide to take time for the group to examine implications of all suggested choices and come to a consensus. If your goal is for students to feel some investment in a decision but also to move the drama forward without delay, you may decide to have them take a vote. When your major goal is to keep the momentum of the activity going, it may be best to make a relatively unimportant decision yourself.

Organizing Groups

To organize students into pairs or small groups, you may find it easiest to let them quickly make their own choices by giving them a task such as "By the time I count to ten, please find a friend and touch elbows with them." Putting a time limitation on choosing groups prevents students from belaboring the process.

In some classes, due to interpersonal issues between students, asking them to choose their own partners or groups can be problematic. In this situation you may want to organize your students into appropriate groupings before the beginning of the lesson and read or post your list as part of preparing for the activity. Another possibility is to draw numbers out of a hat and allow groups to be chosen randomly.

Dividing your class in half can be accomplished simply by drawing an imaginary line through the middle of the group. Or, you may choose to have students count off by 1s and 2s to make the grouping more random. The most important thing to remember in organizing groups is that it should happen quickly and matter-of-factly rather than becoming a major focus of the lesson.

Casting Roles

A special challenge in dramatizing stories or presenting plays with students is casting roles. In casting roles for a story that the class will dramatize several times, choose volunteers for the central roles in the first playing of the story whom you know will model full, enthusiastic participation for the other students. In the second playing of the story, try casting outgoing students alongside shy or more reluctant students in the major roles. It is important to remember that the focus of dramatizing a story is the experience of the participants, not the outward appearance of the product.

When casting a play for informal production, it is best to let students choose their own roles rather than having them audition. Auditioning invites students to compare themselves with others and to focus on their limitations. If several students would like to play the same role, you can pull names from a hat to determine the final casting. Again, it is important to consider who will benefit most from playing a role rather than choosing the child who will perform it the most easily and effectively. It is crucial that the teacher model the attitude that all students are capable of dramatic expression.

Acknowledging Appropriate Behavior

One of the best ways to manage student behavior in any learning situation is to acknowledge appropriate behavior when you see it. It is just as important to praise positive behavior as it is to praise skill and creativity. Your students yearn for your attention. Once they discover that behaving appropriately is the way to get that attention, they will eagerly exhibit the behavior you seek. Comments such as "I really appreciate the way Billy is listening to my directions" or "Susan and Jesse are being very gentle with each other as they move together" lets all of your students know what kind of behavior you value.

Acknowledging appropriate behavior is most effective when it is coupled with ignoring negative behavior. Although it can be extremely difficult to ignore a student who is behaving inappropriately, it is crucial to successful classroom management. Try "catching" a difficult student behaving well—even for a second—and acknowledge him or her immediately.

Dealing with Nonparticipation

A major concern for teachers who have never tried drama activities with their class is that their students "won't do it." Our experience is that children love drama and that most will gladly participate when given an opportunity.

While most children participate in drama readily, it is not uncommon to have one or two students in a class who may initially resist joining in. Sometimes, if a child is timid or shy or comes from a family or cultural background where physical or vocal expression is not encouraged, he or she may feel threatened and overwhelmed when invited to join a drama experience. It is usually best to let such students enter the activity when they feel ready. Allow them to watch for awhile or to take on a responsibility that does not require them to perform in front of others, such as turning on lights or music during an activity. Remember that observing an activity is a form of participation, and even students who are simply watching may be deeply involved.

Another type of nonparticipation stems from a student's desire to enter into a power struggle with you or to impress his peers by being too "cool" to participate. In this case it is best to simply state that participation is mandatory, just as it is for any other classroom activity. Your attitude carries a lot of weight in this situation: If you value drama as much as you value the other curricular subjects, your students are more likely to do so as well.

Guiding the Reluctant Student

The reluctant student is one who participates in drama activities but does not take initiative and tries to remain in the background. It is important to allow such a student to enter the activity at her own pace rather than forcing her to take a more active role. You can begin to get a reluctant student involved in small, relatively nonthreatening ways. For example, a reluctant child could play an important but nonverbal role such as that of someone delivering a message, or a scribe recording the events of the drama.

Guiding the Dominating Student

The dominating student is one who aggressively seeks to control his classmates as well as the direction of a drama activity. The dominating student should be differentiated from the natural leader—someone who is also concerned with bringing out the best in others. The dominating student wants to "run the show," not allowing others the opportunity to express their ideas. One way to handle such a student is to give her a role that requires her to hold back: Perhaps she is the keeper of a secret that may not be divulged to others, or a powerful monarch who commands by gesturing rather than speaking. Note that in these examples the student is given a powerful role rather than a helpless one. Another approach that can be taken in a class with a dominating student is to structure activities in a way that ensures that every child will have an opportunity to contribute. For example, you might go around a circle giving each student a chance to add to a group story rather than having them call out ideas spontaneously.

Encouraging an Appropriate Sound Level

Students will naturally be more verbal when engaging in a drama activity than they are when sitting at their desks listening, reading, or writing. It is necessary and appropriate for them to speak animatedly with one another during a drama session in order to solve problems and collaborate creatively. Therefore, teachers should expect that the classroom sound level during a drama lesson will be higher than at some other times. Many students have difficulty moving their bodies, in particular, without speaking or making sounds. This is partly because the only other time they have a chance to move freely is on the playground where shouting and yelling are the norm. It is also an indicator of the strong developmental connection between the voice and the body and the naturally high energy level of children. Most students simply need training and practice in how to move about the classroom without vocalizing loudly.

It is useful to demonstrate to the class that body movement can provide ways to communicate and express oneself without the need for sound. Ask students to show you a variety of emotions using only their bodies and facial expressions. Encourage them to show the intensity of those feelings without using their voices. For example, "Show me with your body that you are excited...angry...sad...surprised." Last of all, be sure to praise your students whenever they are particularly successful in engaging in a drama lesson with an appropriate sound level.

Motivating Through Drama

Although you may find it challenging, initially, to manage drama activities with your class, over time you will find that drama becomes its own motivation. Your students will want to behave appropriately because they will want you to keep providing them with drama experiences! Letting your students know that their appreciation and enjoyment of drama activities is important to you will ultimately be your most effective management tool.

Chapter Five
CONNECTING DRAMA TO OTHER SUBJECT AREAS

The major goal of this drama curriculum series is to guide teachers in introducing and developing drama skills with their students. However, drama can also be used as a highly effective tool in enhancing learning in other subject areas. This chapter will give you general suggestions in how to use drama to enliven the teaching of Language Arts, Social Studies, Mathematics, Science, Visual Art, and Music in the elementary grades. For specific ideas on integrating the lessons in this Drama Curriculum into other subject areas, see the Variations following each lesson.

Language Arts

Drama offers a rich source of opportunities for deepening and expanding the study of the language arts because both drama and language arts have in common the use of language to communicate and the utilization of character, setting, and other elements of the story form. In addition to the dramatization of poetry and stories, which is covered extensively in the section "Drama and Literature," drama can also be used to enhance the study of Language Arts in the following ways:

1. Movement Activities: Ask students to make the shapes of letters or spell words with their bodies. Groups of children can spell words, each child in the group forming one letter.

2. Pantomime: Have students pantomime as many things as they can think of that begin with a particular letter. If the letter were B, for example, they might pantomime playing baseball,

being bears or birds, blowing up balloons, and so forth. Another pantomime activity is to have students show a verb in pantomime, such as *walking*, then add adverbs such as *softly, bravely, cautiously, excitedly* to the verb and ask them to change their movement accordingly.

3. Playwriting / Dramatization: Have students act out simple stories that they have written individually or as a class.

4. Spontaneous Role Drama: Use improvisational drama to expand on the historical period, setting, or theme of a piece of literature. For example, to prepare students to read or hear a story with the theme of family relationships, have them do a spontaneous role drama in which they have to find a foster family for a child from another planet, leading them to discuss what they think are the important elements of a family.

Foreign Language

Drama activities can give students a motivation for learning and practicing words and phrases in another language.

1. Role Playing / Simulation: Teach students a simple phrase in a foreign language, such as *muchas gracias* (thank you very much—Spanish). Set up an imaginary situation, such as a grocery store where students are shopping, asking questions and buying products. Each student must find at least three occasions to say *muchas gracias* to someone else.

2. Play Production: Many folktales provide natural opportunities for students to learn words, phrases, and even songs in another language. *Multicultural Plays for Children, Volumes 1 and 2* by Pamela Gerke contain many plays that include foreign language.

Social Studies

Engaging in drama activities is a wonderful way to expose children to other cultures and time periods because it allows them to experience being "in another person's skin." Drama enlivens the study of history by infusing past events with the students' own experiences and feelings of the present, thereby helping them realize that history is about real people who had thoughts and feelings much like their own. Drama is also a highly effective way of developing interpersonal skills.

1. Story Dramatization: Have students dramatize folktales from another culture, discussing the differences between that culture and their own.

2. Spontaneous Role Drama: Have students do a role drama that gives them an experience of an essential element of a culture or historical period. Go for a deeply felt feeling of identification rather than an accurate simulation. For example, in preparing students to learn about the American pioneers, have them imagine they are a community of people packing their wagons for a long journey, deciding what to take and what they must leave behind.

3. Improvisation: Use improvised scenarios to explore family and school relationships and to resolve classroom conflicts. An example of this might be having two students do an improvised scene in which one child tries to get the other to give her the answers to a test.

Mathematics

The actual process of solving mathematical problems requires a very different set of skills than the skills used in drama. However, drama can be used to motivate a need for mathematical calculation, as in the story problems in the examples below:

1. Spontaneous Role Drama: The need to do mathematical calculations can be built into a dramatic situation, for example: "We had five water jugs with us when we first became stranded on this desert island. Now three of the jugs are empty. How many jugs do we have left?"

2. Mantle of the Expert: Students as town planners using measurements in scale to map the town, or toy designers working out the correct measurements for the Three Bears' beds.

3. Play Production: "How many centimeters of butcher paper will we need to create a backdrop that covers the blackboard?"

Science

Integrating drama with science can be challenging because science deals with processes, systems, and verifiable facts whereas drama tends to deal more with the human experience. There are ways, however, to give students an experience of scientific phenomena through drama:

1. Movement Activities: Movement can be used to help students imagine such natural forces as gravity, states of matter, and magnetic attraction. For detailed lessons that integrate movement with earth science, see Helen Landalf's *Moving the Earth: Teaching Earth Science Through Movement in Grades 3–6.*

2. Spontaneous Role Drama: Students can explore science topics by taking an imaginary role that will motivate learning. For example in studying weather, students might take on the role of scientists who shrink themselves so they can enter droplets of water and experience evaporation and precipitation.

3. Mantle of the Expert: Create situations where students need scientific information to solve problems that they, as "experts"

in a particular field, have been presented with. For example, perhaps they are agricultural engineers who need to create an irrigation system for an imaginary village. To fulfill this role they will need to gather information on the role of water and soil in the growth of plants.

Visual Art

Drama provides opportunities for students to both practice and appreciate the visual arts.

1. Playwriting, Dramatization: Show students realistic or abstract works of art and have them create stories based on what they see. The stories could be verbalized, written, or dramatized.

2. Movement Activities: Have students create "sculptures" with their bodies, or dance their impressions of realistic or abstract works of art.

3. Play Production: Involve students in designing and constructing sets, props, and costumes for an informal play production.

Music

Music and drama make excellent companions because music evokes mood, which can find its expression in drama.

1. Movement activities/Pantomime: Play a piece of music for students and ask them to imagine a setting, character, or situation that the music suggests to them. They could then express their ideas through movement and pantomime. For example, play short selections of music of different kinds and have students enter the playing area one at a time, walking as the character each type of music suggests to them.

2. Dramatization/Play Production: Have students use musical instruments to create sounds for a story dramatization or informal play production. They can also play live or recorded music during the transitions between scenes of a play.

Physical Education and Dance

Physical action is a major element in drama, and therefore many connections can be drawn between drama and physical education, particularly dance.

1. Movement Activities: Many of the activities in this curriculum that are geared toward the development of body awareness and movement skills can also be used in physical education or dance lessons by focusing on the movement itself rather than on the activity's dramatic context. For example, by de-emphasizing its Postal Service context, the activity "Body Part Isolation: Warm-Ups" in Lesson 1 could be used to explore moving and body part awareness in an introductory physical education or dance lesson.

2. Pantomime: Exaggerating the movements of a pantomime can lead to the creation of a dance. Ask your students to pantomime an activity, then make their movements larger and larger until their entire bodies are involved. Playing background music will help students make the transition from pantomime to dance.

3. Play Production: Dances can be included in informal play productions. If performing a folktale from another culture, teach your students a traditional folk dance, or create your own folk-style dance to music of that culture. It is also possible to have students choreograph their own dances to perform as part of a play.

Chapter Six
STARTING OUT:
CREATING A CONTEXT

The teacher who uses this curriculum will be providing his students with a unique experience because these students will have the opportunity to learn and practice the skills and techniques of drama not by doing a series of unrelated exercises, but rather by engaging in activities within an overall dramatic context. Such an approach increases the students' motivation and involvement, and it gives a sense of purpose to each drama lesson. You, as the teacher, must first establish the overall context of the curriculum before Lesson 1 even begins. Creating the context will require two or three class periods of approximately 15–30 minutes each, preferably occurring over consecutive days.

Mail and Mystery, Families and Friends, requires that students initially embrace the role of being members of a Stamp and Sticker Design Company who enter a competition to design a postage stamp series with the theme "Honoring Postal Workers." We suggest that you create the initial scenario by following the steps outlined below.

Step 1: Exploration (optional)

Materials / Preparation:
- Materials for a Stamp and Sticker Exploration Station, including some or all of the following:
  - Stamps and stickers of all kinds: postage stamps, rubber stamps, decorative stickers, and so on
  - Stamp pads and paper
  - Blank stickers (such as self-stick computer mailing labels)
  - Pens and markers
  - A stamp collection, posters of postage stamp designs, and so forth

A few days before you plan to start using this curriculum, create a Stamp and Sticker Exploration Station by placing all the materials listed above on tables. Allow students plenty of free time to look at the stamps and stickers and to experiment with the materials. This can happen in one activity period or over several days. You can also ask students to bring their own stamps and stickers to class.

Step 2: Discussion / Initiating Ownership in the Enterprise

After all students have had the opportunity to explore the Stamp and Sticker Station, hold a class discussion about stamps and stickers (or, if you did not create an Exploration Station, simply initiate the discussion by showing your class examples of various stamps and stickers). Ask students what they know about stamps and stickers, their designs, and the process for manufacturing them. Ask questions such as:

"Why do you think they chose to make this particular picture?"

"What do you know about the subject of this stamp design?"

"What do these particular stamps have in common? How are they different?"

"How do they make paper sticky on one side? Where could we find out this information?"

"Who do you think chooses the subjects for the stamps or stickers?"

"Where do you suppose stamp and sticker designers get their ideas?"

"What skills would a person need to have in order to be a stamp designer?"

As teacher, participate in the discussion as someone who is also curious about stamps and stickers. Do not participate as "the one who knows"; that is, do not act as an authority who provides factual information to fill in any gaps in students' understanding. It is crucial that you establish from the very beginning of this curriculum that you are present as a *facilitator* of your students' learning process, not as an *authority* who judges their responses (the traditional teaching model). This initial stage is one in which you begin to engage students in the dramatic context; it is not intended to be a factual seminar on stamp and sticker production.

After ideas and information about the topic have been discussed, present the idea that the class itself could be members of a Stamp and Sticker Design Company. Say something like:

> "*You know, if we wanted to, we could be a company that designs stamps and stickers... I don't suppose it would be too difficult to think up designs and draw them...do you think we could do that?*"

> "*If we were a stamp a sticker design company, what would our name be?*"

Ask students to suggest names for your company and write their suggestions on the board. Each name will carry implications for the type of stamp and sticker design company it represents. Point out the implications of each name so that students can make informed decisions about the kind of company they would like to establish. For example: "World Stickers" carries the implication that this company has international connections; "Mickey Mouse's Stickers" implies that the company is associated with the Disney Corporation; "Stickers R Us" implies that the company designs toy-related stickers. Together with your class, decide which name the class will adopt for their design company. Agreement can be arrived at by voting or by general consensus.

Step 3: Business as Usual

MATERIALS / PREPARATION:

- Before students arrive, create a sign—either on cardboard or on the blackboard—with these words:

(The name of your class's Stamp and Sticker Design Company)
Studio A

- A supply of paper and pencils, enough for each student, placed on a table somewhere.

- Certificates of Design Awards, taped to the wall. These need not be elaborate nor look highly authentic—simply write them with pen or markers on plain pieces of paper. Some examples:

DESIGN OF THE YEAR AWARD TO:
name of your Stamp and Sticker Design Company
(Dated 2 years ago)

CERTIFICATE OF EXCELLENCE
"MOST CREATIVE DESIGN"
To: *name of your Stamp and Sticker Design Company*
(dated 10 years ago)

- The Stamp and Sticker Exploration Station can be left as is, perhaps as a company resource center or storeroom

- (Optional) You may choose to move your classroom furniture around a bit to create a new look for the company design studio.

- (Optional) Engage students in a discussion and decision about the kind of furniture layout their studio should have. Ask students questions such as: "What kind of furniture and equipment will we need? How should we set up our work space? Where will our supplies be located?" and so on.

PROCEDURE:

When students arrive (such as after a recess), immediately assume your role as the Company Secretary. This is a role that will allow you to offer assistance to the "designers" without being their boss—it will be more empowering to students if you are not in a role of high authority. (You can also choose another role with a similar stance, such as Receptionist or Clerk.) Say something to students to signal to them that they are now in the world of the Design Company, for example: *"Welcome back to work, Designers! While you were out, a new order for stamp designs arrived. Oh, and UPS came with the shipment of pencils. I put them in the storeroom."* (Indicate the area where you've placed the supply of pencils and paper.)

At this initial phase of creating the context of the Design Company, engage students in the task of drawing stamps and stickers. Doing actual tasks will give your students a concrete way of transitioning to the drama of the Design Company. In role drama, this transition is called a "point of entry." Help students get started by having them select a subject for their drawings. You can do this in role as their Secretary by saying things such as the following:

> *"Now someone remind me—which of you are working on designing stickers for that toy company? Why don't you sit together over by the window."*

> *"Who is designing those baseball stamps? Remember, our client wants the designs by the end of the week"*

> *"We just got a new order for stickers of ships and airplanes—who will draw the designs?"*

In addition to drawing stamp and sticker designs, students may want to improvise other (pantomime) tasks, such as answering the company phone, making photocopies, or sending faxes. This is fine as it indicates that students are engaged in the make-believe world of the design studio.

You can indirectly let students know what your own role is by saying something like: *"After working here for so many years as your secretary, you would think I would know the phone number for*

FedEx by heart!" You do not need to be an actor when "in role"—it's enough for you to convey the attitudes appropriate to your role as company secretary (or whatever role you choose). It's perfectly all right for you to come "out of role" at any time to explain matters to students as their teacher—students will have no problem transitioning between the "real world" and the imaginary world of this business enterprise.

Establish the fact that your company has a long history of success and expertise by posting the award certificates and by saying such things as, "This is how we've always done it" or, "In all these years of business, I don't think we've had this kind of design order before." It's also important that your business operation is one in which the staff members work cooperatively and efficiently to deliver quality goods. Avoid the creation of antagonistic relationships, such as battles between management and workers or with business competitors (see Commentary, below).

Avoid using actual items as props—such as a real or toy telephone. Students are entering the world of their Design Company *in their minds* and will use their "drama eyes" to see the objects, places and even some of the people that they encounter along the way. To encourage imaginative visualization, indicate objects necessary to the operation of your business with pantomime or by using simple paper representations. For example, a piece of paper with the telephone keypad drawn on it can indicate the telephone.

Step 4: Receiving the Challenge

Materials / Preparation:
- Photocopy the following "electronic message" on a single sheet of paper or create your own message, if desired. Fill in: 1) the name of your design company (as the recipient of the message); 2) the current date; and 3) the deadline date. Set the deadline for a date at which time you expect to have completed Lesson 13. (If your schedule changes later, you can simply notify students at that time of a change in the deadline date. Note: this e-mail address is entirely fictitious.)

e-mail message...

From: <u>postmaster.general@usa.com</u>

To: _____

Date: _____

Your company has been chosen, as one of the three top stamp and sticker design companies in this country, to enter a contest to design a new postage stamp series.

The theme of this stamp series is:

Honoring U.S. Postal Workers

Designs must show the work of U.S. Postal Workers and how this work serves the community by bringing families together.

The deadline for design proposals is: _____

Please respond within 2 working days.

(Failure to reply will result in noncompliance, as per Government Regulation #295726-XPPG.98-HL13)

Postmaster General
United States Postal Service

_____

After your students have spent some time in role as the Designers, drawing stamps and stickers (during one or more class periods), you will be ready to introduce this e-mail message. You can ask someone, such as a member of your school's office staff or a parent volunteer, to deliver the e-mail message during a time when students are working in their Company Studio, or you can simply announce to students that this message has arrived. Call everyone together for a "staff meeting" and read the message aloud to them.

Step 5: Discussing the Proposal

Immediately after reading the message hold a general discussion—in role as members of the design company—on the question of whether or not the company should enter the competition. Encourage students to thoroughly examine the idea, asking them such questions as, "What would be the pros and cons of taking on this project? Do we have room on our upcoming work schedule to do this proposal justice? Are we capable of doing this job well?" Remind them that your company has never before designed postage stamps and that they will have to do a lot of research on postal workers.

Although your students are sure to be highly enthusiastic about taking on this project, some students may wonder if the e-mail message is "real." At no time during this curriculum will you attempt to fool your students into believing something that isn't true. As drama artists they will be creating their own imaginary world and will have no trouble transitioning between the real and the pretend (children are expert at this). If you have any cynics in your class, frankly admit that the e-mail message is make-believe and ask them, "But are you willing to believe it's real?" Establishing belief in the dramatic context is one of your principle concerns during this initial phase of the curriculum.

Step 6: Responding to the Proposal

The final step your students need to take before they embark on Lesson 1 of this curriculum is to respond to the e-mail message from the Postmaster General. Before ending your staff meeting, ask the Designers to dictate a reply to you (their secretary). Write down students' ideas as they speak. As their reply takes shape, periodically read it back to students while raising the standard of their language by using proper English and grammar. Adding a formal, professional veneer to their words will upgrade the drama and help to make it more believable. For example, if students say, "Ask how much they'll pay!" you can read the draft back to them as, "Upon the matter of payment, we would appreciate an estimate for fees." Rather than correcting students' language as they speak, allow students to experience proper language and sentence structure by hearing it read to them.

When the reply is completed, assure the Designers that you will send it electronically. You are now ready to begin Lesson 1 of *Mail and Mystery, Families and Friends.*

COMMENTARY:

The dramatic context of this curriculum makes use of a classroom drama technique called "Mantle of the Expert." This exciting, effective and deeply creative technique, pioneered by British drama educator Dorothy Heathcote, can be extended far beyond the application in this book. Gavin Bolton, a drama-in-education expert and author of several books on the subject, writes, "I am now convinced that Mantle of the Expert is the most sophisticated and enlightened approach to education to have been devised and that future generations will benefit from its philosophy and practice." *(Drama for Learning* by Dorothy Heathcote and Gavin Bolton)

One important point to make here about this particular technique is with regard to creating dramatic tension. Although tension is often created in drama and theater by establishing conflict, in Mantle of the Expert, dramatic tension is created by the need for the "experts" to deliver satisfaction to their "clients." Dorothy Heathcote views this as a moral consideration. Rather than focusing the drama on hostility, power, inadequacies, abuses, and repression, she "...wants our children to have the fulfilling experience, however briefly, of creating a fictional society that cooperates, takes responsibilities, sets high standards of achievement, brings out the best in everyone through committed endeavor. The enterprise world within a world offers them a vision of the possible." (*Drama For Learning*)

Although the emphasis of this curriculum is on the development of drama skills, the context also makes it rich in possibilities for learning in other subject areas, especially as it relates not only to the subject of design (art and drawing, measurement, research, writing ideas and proposals, and so forth) but also postal services (measurement, sorting and counting, identifying numbers and letters, geography of routes, social skills, current events, and so on), as well as the broader topic of family and community (social studies, civics, history, and so forth). We recommend that you provide learning opportunities on these and other connected topics concurrently with the presentation of this drama curriculum, and that you make resources available to students in the form of books, videos, pictures, guest speakers, and field trips.

PART II
EXPLORATION AND RESEARCH
ON POSTAL WORKERS

Now that you have created a dramatic context with your class, you can begin to build your student's drama skills within that context. The following set of lessons focus your students on observing and participating in the work and family lives of Postal Workers. Students, in their role as Stamp Designers, tour the Postal Workers Training School and the Post Office, go out in the field with Mail Carriers, and visit the homes of Postal Workers.

Within the context of researching Postal Workers for their postage stamp designs, students will be introduced to some of the basic tools of drama. They will practice concentration (essential to dramatic imagining) and observation, and they will engage in activities to increase body awareness and develop creative expression through movement. They will explore using their voices expressively and will experience working cooperatively with others (artistic collaboration). They will practice the basic drama skills of pantomime, improvisation, and story creation.

Lesson 1
The Postal Workers' Training School

    A. Body Part Isolation: *Warm-Ups*   (5 minutes)
    B. Visual Observation: *What's Different?*   (10 minutes)
    C. Sorting and Sequencing: *Line Up!*   (10–15 minutes)

(Note: For this lesson, as for any lessons in this curriculum, you may choose to extend the activities over two or three lesson periods. You may repeat these activities at any time throughout the course of this curriculum.)

A. Body Part Isolation: *Warm-Ups*

CONTEXT:
"In order to create postage stamp designs on the theme of 'Honoring Postal Workers,' we must first research our topic. Today we will visit the Postal Workers' Training School.

Mail carriers must be in top physical condition in order to make their deliveries. Our first stop at the Training School will be the gym, where postal workers get into shape."

SKILLS:
Awareness and control of body parts

MATERIALS / PREPARATION:
- Make a sign on cardboard or write on the blackboard the following words:

US POSTAL WORKERS TRAINING SCHOOL
Visitors: Please sign in at the front desk

- For this lesson, as for all movement activities in this curriculum, you will need an open area in your classroom where students can move freely. Move furniture as needed. Initially, students will sign in (pantomime) at the "front desk," which can simply be your own desk or a table.

- We encourage teachers to always do movement activities along with their students. (For the first activity, "Warm-Ups," women teachers will need to wear pants.) In order to make it easier to speak the words of this activity while doing the movements, we recommend you do one of the following: Photocopy the text of "Warm-Ups" (to make it easier to handle), write the words on the blackboard, or memorize it.

PROCEDURE:

1. Inform students that their Design Company will now visit the Postal Workers Training School. Post the Training School sign and read it aloud. Tell students they must sign in at the "front desk" (indicate your desk or other location in the room) after which they should meet you in the Training School "gym" (indicate the movement area of your room).

   Demonstrate: Walk to the "front desk," pantomime signing a guest register, then go to the movement area and sit down. Students should then do the same. When they sit, have them spread themselves out in the movement area.

2. Tell students to make sure that they are far enough away from others so that, when seated, they can stretch their arms and legs wide, as in the letter *X* (demonstrate if needed).

   Explain to students that this activity will take place in Self Space, meaning that they will stay in one spot without touching anyone else and without traveling through the room. Students begin seated, cross-legged, while facing you.

3. Read the following series of "Warm-Ups" while you and your students do the described movements.

WARM-UPS by Pamela Gerke, with Helen Landalf

1. Stretching

Repeat this poem several times. It's fine if students say the words along with you. Optional: Sing this poem—see music at the end of this lesson.

Take a deep breath...	*inhale slowly*
Give a big sigh...	*exhale slowly*
Stretch your <u>fingers</u> far	*reach hands and fingers in front of you*
Stretch your <u>fingers</u> high	*raise hands and fingers straight up overhead*
Float those <u>fingers</u> right	*slowly bring hands and arms down*
Down from the sky!	*toward the floor*
Swish, Swish, Swish, Swish	*in soft, wavelike motions*
Take a deep breath...	
Give a big sigh...	
Stretch your <u>shoulders</u> 'round	*make circles with shoulders*
Stretch your <u>shoulders</u> high	*raise shoulders toward the ceiling*
Shake those <u>shoulders</u> right	
Down from the sky!	*wiggle shoulders as you slowly lower them to*
Shh, Shh, Shh, Shh	*normal position*
Take a deep breath...	
Give a big sigh...	
Stretch your <u>legs</u> far	*spread legs out to the sides*
Stretch your <u>legs</u> high	*bring legs together and lift them up toward the ceiling*
Fly those legs right	*while leaning back on forearms and elbows*
Down from the sky!	

Rrr, Rrr, Rrr, Rrr
(airplane sounds)

slowly lower legs to floor is soft,
wavelike motions

Take a deep breath...
Give a big sigh...
Stretch your <u>eyeballs</u> far

"bug" eyes outward

Stretch your <u>eyeballs</u> high

look up toward the ceiling without
tilting head back

Blink those <u>eyeballs</u> right
Down from the sky!

blink eyes as you lower them to
normal position

Blink, Blink, Blink, Blink

Take a deep breath...
Give a big sigh...
Stretch your <u>tongue</u> far

stick out tongue

Stretch your <u>tongue</u> high

raise tongue toward the ceiling
without tilting head

Wiggle that <u>tongue</u> right
Down from the sky!

wiggle tongue as you lower it and
put it back inside your mouth

Ulul, Ulul, Ulul, Ulul
(tongue wiggle sounds)

Slowly:
Take a deep breath...
Give a big sigh...
Stretch your <u>body</u> far

stretch arms and legs away from
your body

Stretch your <u>body</u> high

stand up on tiptoes, stretch arms
up overhead

Melt your <u>body</u> right
Down from the sky!

gently moving body from side to
side, slowly "fall" to
the floor

Ahh, Ahh, Ahh, Ahh

2. Calisthenics

Remain seated on the floor, legs straight in front of you. To begin: Bend knees while you support yourself with your hands at your sides. Do each exercise SLOWLY.

Heels do push-ups
Off the floor!
Count to four: 1-2-3-4   *keeping balls of feet on the floor, lift heels on each count*

Palms do push-ups   *sit cross-legged and place palms on floor in front of you*
Off the floor!   *keeping fingertips on the floor,*
Count to four: 1-2-3-4   *raise palms up and lower them to the floor on each count*

Jumping jacks to
Make arms fit!   *stretch arms out to sides*
Count to six: 1-2-3-4-5-6   *raise arms up and clap hands overhead on each count*

Jumping jacks to   *with your hands on the floor*
Make legs fit!   *behind you for support,*
Count to six: 1-2-3-4-5-6   *gently clap legs together in mid-air on each count*

For pull-ups for your knees,   *with your hands still behind you for support, bend knees and,*
Take this position, please: *while keeping them together,*
Count to eight: 1-2-3-4-5-6-7-8 *shift them from side to side on each count*

For pull-ups for your chin
Please don't smile or grin!
Count to eight: 1-2-3-4-5-6-7-8 *raise up and lower chin on each count, moving head freely up and down*

See if you can match my pace
While your <u>toes</u> jog in place · · · · *stretch legs out in front*
of you again
Count to eight: 1-2-3-4-5-6-7-8 · *wiggle toes swiftly while counting*

See if you can match my pace
While your <u>elbows</u> jog in place · *bend elbows and place hands*
on shoulders
Count to eight: 1-2-3-4-5-6-7-8 · *move elbows swiftly while counting*

Last of all: a side bend · · · · · · · *arch right arm over your head and*
gently bend to the left. Repeat with
the opposite side: With left arm
overhead, bend to the right
Our Warm-Ups now
Are at an end!

COMMENTARY:
Physical warm-ups are basic to the development of drama skills for
they focus students' attention on their bodies—their principal instrument of expression—and help students gain control over their movements. The first part of this activity also includes breathing, for the
purpose of both relaxation and body/breath awareness. When you
stretch your jaw and tongue, your words will naturally sound
funny—students will enjoy this and will know the poem well enough
at that point to understand what you are saying (or singing).

This activity introduces students to the concept of Self Space, the
space directly around one's body. When moving in Self Space one
does not travel. This activity also requires students to identify various body parts and move them in isolation. Use these warm-ups at
anytime throughout this curriculum or any other part of your school
day, especially when your students are restless or need to focus their
energy.

VARIATIONS:

Add other body parts to these warm-ups (don't worry about making everything rhyme). Along with large body parts—such as legs, arms, torso—don't neglect face, mouth, ears, cheeks, neck, throat, knuckles, wrists, ankles. Ask students for their ideas for body-part exercises. Together, the class can create rhymes to go along with the warm-ups. For example, if someone suggests "feet," ask students for words that rhyme, such as: *neat, sweet, heat.* Your class might then create this rhyme: "Rub your feet / And feel the heat."

Stretching

Take a deep breath *(inhale slowly)* Give a big sigh *(exhale slowly)* Stretch your

fin - gers	far		Stretch your	fin - gers	high
shoul - ders	'round			shoul - ders	
legs	far			legs	-
eye - balls	far			eye - balls	
tongue	far			tongue	-
bo - dy	far			bo - dy	

Float	those	fin - gers	right	down from the sky!
Shake	those	shoul - ders		
Fly	those	legs		
Blink	those	eyes		
Wiggle	that	tongue		
Melt	that	bo - dy		

	Swish,	Swish,	Swish,	Swish,	Swish....
	Shh,	Shh,	Shh,	Shh,	Shh....
(airplane)	Rrr,	Rrr,	Rrr,	Rrr,	Rrr....
	Blink,	Blink,	Blink,	Blink,	Blink....
(tongue wiggle)	Ulul,	Ulul,	Ulul,	Ulul,	Ulul....
	Ahh,	Ahh,	Ahh,	Ahh,	Ahh....

B. Visual Observation:
What's Different?

CONTEXT:
"Postal workers must have good observational skills in order to correctly read the addresses on letters and to deliver them to the right places."

SKILLS:
Use and development of powers of observation and awareness of details

MATERIALS / PREPARATION:
- Make 3–4 pairs of nearly identical "envelopes." Students will be examining each pair to determine what is different.
  - Use blank paper or card stock in rectangles of approximately 25 x 35cm (approx. 10" x 14").
  - On each "envelope" write a simple, fictitious recipient address, return address, and draw a postage stamp.
  - Make each pair of envelopes exactly the same except for one detail, such as inverting a number or adding a letter.
  - Write letters and numbers large enough so that all students will be able to read them from a distance.
  - Make each envelope address as simple or complex as needed to suit the learning needs of your students.

Example:

123 Drama Rd.   (stamp drawing)
Seattle, WA

           The Cats
           45 A Street
           Purr City, CA 99991

(On the other copy of this envelope, change "A St." to "B St.")

- Students will need to be seated facing you, so that all will be able to see the envelopes.

PROCEDURE:
1. Tell students that they will be examining pairs of envelopes in order to determine what is different about each pair. Hold up one of your sample envelopes and ask students to silently examine it for about 30 seconds.

2. While still holding up this first envelope, also hold up its partner envelope and ask students to say what is different about the second one. Students may say their ideas aloud.

3. Repeat the procedure with all the other sample envelope pairs you have made. If your students are quick to discern the differences between envelope addresses, challenge them by putting the first envelope face down when you hold up the second one so that they must use their memories.

COMMENTARY:
This activity is a classic drama education game that helps develop observational skills.

Students will enjoy the challenge it provides while they simultaneously practice letter and number recognition. You can make the envelope addresses as simple or complex as needed to challenge the reading level of your students.

VARIATIONS:
If you repeat this activity periodically throughout the school year, you can increase the complexity of the challenge by creating more than one difference between each envelope pair. Students can also be challenged to create their own nearly identical pairs of envelopes. Students pass their own envelope pairs to other students who then try to figure out the differences.

You can also do the "What's Different?" game with the physical appearance of individuals. Have a volunteer stand in front of the class and ask students to closely examine their appearance and notice every detail about their clothing, hair, and so forth. After about 30 seconds, the volunteer leaves the room and alters one detail of their appearance, such as unbuttoning a button or untying a shoelace. The volunteer then comes back into the room and students say aloud what has changed about their appearance.

C. Sorting and Sequencing: *Line Up!*

Thanks to Clayton Miller.

CONTEXT:

"Postal workers need to be able to sort the names and addresses on letters and put them in order. We will practice putting alphabet letters and numbers in the correct order."

SKILLS:

Collaboration with others

MATERIALS / PREPARATION:

- You will need a set of playing cards. Remove the court cards (Jacks, Queens, and Kings) and the Joker. Shuffle the deck.

- Before students arrive, determine where in your room students will be able to stand comfortably in a single line. Decide where students at the beginning of the lineup will be (representing either the letter A or the number 1) and where students at the end of the lineup will be (representing the letter Z or the number 10)

PROCEDURE:

1. The class can remain where they are as you welcome students to the Letter Sorting Workshop. Tell them that in this workshop they will practice putting both alphabet letters and numbers in proper order.

   First, students will arrange themselves in a row in alphabetical order of the first letter of their first names. If two or more students' names begin with the same letter, they will then line up according to the second letter of their names (for example: Katie, Kerry, Kevin), resorting to the third letter if needed (Kathy, Katie, Katrina).

2. Tell students they will have until the count of 15 to line up in alphabetical order. Show students where a person whose first name begins with the letter A will stand (or whichever is the

first alphabet letter of your students' names) and where the person will stand whose first letter of their first name is closest to the end of the alphabet.

3. Say, "Ready, Go: 1...2..."(and so on) Count aloud slowly from 1 to 15, at a speed at which students barely have time to complete the lineup. Except for counting, don't say anything, so that students must interact with each other in order to figure out the correct lineup. (Saying "Ready, Go:" helps students get prepared for the start of the count. In music, this is, in fact, called a "preparatory" signal.)

4. When students have completed the lineup, together recite aloud all students' first names, in alphabetical order. If needed, ask students as a group to identify and correct any errors in alphabetizing in the lineup.

6. Repeat step 3–4 of the procedure, but this time students line up in the alphabetical order of the first letter of their last names.

7. Inform students that postal workers, when sorting letters, must also be able to put numbers in correct numerical order. Tell students that you will give each of them a playing card and they will then line up in the numerical order of their cards.

   Explain that the numbers on the cards will range from 1 (Ace) to 10. Where the letter A stood in your alphabetical lineup, students with Ace cards will now stand; whereas students with number 10 cards will stand where the end of the alphabet stood before.

8. Randomly pass out the playing cards (minus the court cards). Repeat steps 3–4 of the procedure and this time, students must line up in the numerical order of their cards. Students with the same numbers can simply stand next to each other in the lineup.

9. If desired, you can repeat the numerical lineup one or more times. To do so, collect the cards, shuffle them and then randomly pass them out again.

COMMENTARY:

Working cooperatively together to form the lineup in correct order is a good beginning activity in concentration and collaboration. Students must interact with each other to solve the problem and must create the correct lineup in a limited amount of time, thereby requiring them to focus their attention.

VARIATIONS:

Students can also make shapes together using their bodies to create various patterns on the floor. For example, "By the time I finish counting to 15, you will together create a large square (or triangle, rectangle, oval, and so forth)." Students then arrange themselves in the pattern you have named. It's important that you not interfere and direct students in this activity, thereby forcing them to collaborate and think for themselves.

Lesson 2
At the Post Office

A. Pantomime: *Imaginary Packages*   (10 minutes)
B. Improvisation: *Gibberish*   (10 minutes)
C. Movement Activity: *Movement Machine*   (10 minutes)

A. Pantomime: *Imaginary Packages*

CONTEXT:
"Postal workers must handle packages of many different weights, shapes, and sizes."

SKILLS:
Expressive use of body and movement
Use and development of flexible thinking and spontaneity

MATERIALS / PREPARATION:
- Set up your classroom, or an area of your classroom, as the Post Office. For this you will need:
  - "U.S. Post Office" written on the blackboard or on a cardboard sign hung on the wall
  - A table or desk at the front of the room to simulate a counter
  - Enough empty space for students to line up at the counter and to later engage in a movement activity (see Activity C, "Movement Machine)
- Students begin standing in a circle.

PROCEDURE:
1. Tell students that part of a postal worker's job is to handle packages of many different sizes, shapes, and weights. Explain to students that you will describe an imaginary package—its size, shape, weight, or contents. You will pick up this imaginary package and pass it to the student on your right. Students will pass

this imaginary package around the circle. Each student must receive the package and pass it to the next person while pantomiming the characteristics of the package—its size, shape, and weight.

2. Say the following description: "small jewelry box." Pantomime carefully picking up a small box from the floor, then placing it gently in the hands of the student on your right, who then passes it to the next student and so on around the circle. Encourage students to feel the size, shape, and weight of the package as they lift it, and to show these characteristics with their movements.

3. When the package returns to you, repeat the procedure using the suggested descriptions below. You may also add descriptions of your own.
   long, rectangular box containing barbells (weights)
   small, soft, squishy package
   large, spherical package (such as might contain a soccer
       or basketball)
   gigantic box of feathers
   box containing a live animal, with a carrying handle
   medium-sized box of delicate china

COMMENTARY:

This activity provides an experience in the central dramatic concept of using the imagination to create something that isn't really there. Creating a single imaginary object—a package—provides a foundation for the more complex imaginative experiences to come, when students will be called upon to interact with many imaginary objects and settings and to believe strongly in premises that they create in their own minds.

Pantomime is the expression of an idea, feeling, intention, or situation through action without the use of the voice; it is a primary drama skill. Begin this activity slowly, encouraging students to see and believe in the properties of each imaginary package and to show those properties in the way they handle the package with their hands and arms, and perhaps through their facial expressions. Point out to them that they must keep the size, shape, and weight of a package consistent as they pass it along to the next person. If a student does not appear to be concentrating on miming the package appropriately, stop and ask her to repeat the task with a focus on the properties of the package.

VARIATIONS:
Focus on descriptive vocabulary by asking students to think of other phrases that could describe a package. Write the phrases on the blackboard as you repeat them aloud, then use those phrases in the activity. Encourage students to think of opposites such as big and little, heavy and light, soft and hard. Also encourage them to think divergently by suggesting unusual package characteristics (hot, cold, slimy, prickly, and so on).

After doing this activity several times with each student passing the same package, you can add the challenge of asking each student to pantomime a change in the size, shape, or weight of the package before they pass it to the next person. Students will also enjoy tossing the packages to each other across the circle, calling out the name of the person who is to catch the package.

B. Improvisation: *Gibberish*

CONTEXT:
"The people who work at the Post Office counter are experts at interacting with the public. Each day, they must answer questions and solve problems for many people."

SKILLS:
Expressive use of voice and nonverbal communication
Use and development of flexible thinking and spontaneity

MATERIALS / PREPARATION:
   Set up a Post Office counter, as described in Activity A, "Imaginary Packages"

PROCEDURE:
   1. Discuss with students the fact that people come into the Post Office with many different attitudes and feelings. For example, someone might come in hopeful that they will receive an important letter, angry because a package got lost, or sad because a letter they were expecting didn't come. Ask students to suggest other situations that might cause customers to come into the Post Office with a particular feeling or attitude.

   2. Explain to students that when you speak with sounds that aren't real words it's called speaking in "gibberish." Demonstrate this by saying a few gibberish phrases, for example: "Blagabeed hoogala!" "Jeerish hoonik sabit?"

   3. Tell the students that you will now ask them a question in gibberish, and that they are to reply, also in gibberish. Now do so, making sure to put the inflection of a question in your voice. Allow them to reply as a group. Next, reverse roles by having them ask you a question in gibberish to which you reply.

4. Now ask students, as a group, to do the following:
   - Tell me, in gibberish, that you are angry because the Post Office lost an important package that you wanted delivered.
   - Tell me, in gibberish, that you are sad because your best friend moved away and you can't find his address.
   - Tell me, in gibberish, that you are frightened because a strange person followed you to the Post Office.

5. Choose a student volunteer for the following demonstration: Tell the students that you are now a person working behind the counter at the Post Office. When the customer (the volunteer) comes to the counter (your desk or a table), you will whisper to them why they have come to the Post Office and how they are feeling. Then you will ask aloud, in gibberish, "May I help you?" The volunteer is to reply to you in gibberish, using her voice to show how she is feeling. After the customer has finished speaking, you will reply briefly to her comment. For example:

   > Teacher: *(You, whispering)*: You are angry because an important letter is lost.
   > Postal Worker: *(You)* Bagabooga Deeshee? *May I help you?*
   > Customer: *(Student volunteer, angrily)* Von gona looba dit! *The Post Office lost my letter!*
   > Postal Worker: Toolooshin nea fela code. *I'm sorry, we'll take care of it right away.*

   After this exchange, ask the class to guess what feeling or attitude the customer had. Your response as the Postal Worker can be neutral or can match the attitude of the customer.

6. Select five to ten students to form a line at the "counter," repeating the sequence in Step 3 above with each student. When all students in line have interacted with you, ask them to take their seats. Select another group of students to line up as customers. Repeat this improvisation as many times as desired, ideally giving each student in the class a turn as a customer. See list

below for suggestions of feelings and motivations to whisper to students:

- You're *sad* because a letter from your friend has not arrived.
- You're *scared* because you think someone followed you into the Post Office.
- You're *worried* because you don't have enough money to send an important package.
- You're *nervous* because you want to ask for a job at the Post Office.
- You're *happy* because you're expecting a big birthday package.

COMMENTARY:

Speaking in gibberish is an excellent activity for encouraging vocal inflection and variation because students cannot rely on the meaning of their words to get a message across. Although some students may initially feel self-conscious about speaking in gibberish, with practice most will come to enjoy it immensely.

A common mistake when first attempting to speak gibberish is to make it sound like a particular language, using the inflections of German, Japanese, Italian, and so forth. This is to be avoided not only because it encourages stereotypical ethnic characterizations but because gibberish sounds need to be as unrelated to a real language as possible in order to accomplish the goal of pressing students to convey meaning through their voices rather than to rely on words.

VARIATIONS:

If your class is ready to work independently, you can have students do this activity in groups of five or six. One student in each group will play the Postal Worker and the remaining students will play customers. The "customers" decide for themselves what feeling or attitude they will express through gibberish. When the Postal Worker has interacted with each of the customers, another student in the group becomes the Postal Worker. You can circulate among the groups providing assistance as needed.

For fun, try using gibberish at other times in the classroom. For example, you might have students recite a favorite poem in gibberish.

Or, if the attention of your students is wandering, give a direction in gibberish and challenge them to figure out what you are asking them to do.

C. Movement Activity:
Movement Machine

CONTEXT:
"Let's work together to show some of the machines that might be used at the Post Office."

SKILLS:
Awareness and control of body parts
Collaboration and negotiation with others

MATERIALS / PREPARATION:
- CD player or tape deck (optional)
- Adequate space for each student to move in place without touching another person

MUSICAL SUGGESTIONS:
Chappelle, Eric, "Add On Machine," *Music for Creative Dance: Contrast and Continuum, Volume I.*
(This activity may also be presented without music.)

PROCEDURE:
1. Ask students to find empty places to stand and to imagine that each of their bodies is one part of a big machine. (This may also be done with only half or a third of the class moving at once.) Each machine part will have one simple movement that it repeats over and over. Demonstrate several simple, repetitive movements that can be done without traveling, such as moving an arm forward and backwards or twisting the body from side to side. Ask students to try out several simple, repetitive movements of their own choosing. Some students may naturally add a sound to their movement, which is fine.

2. Tell the class that they will now create a machine together that does a job in the Post Office. It might be a mail-sorting machine,

a stamping machine, or any other machine that the students decide on. The machine could be real or imaginary. Ask students for suggestions of what kind of machine they would like to create, then together discuss the suggestions and decide on one of them. (See the section on "Facilitating Group Decision Making" in Chapter 4 for suggestions on guiding students in this process.)

3. Call on one student to come to the center of the room and begin a repetitive movement. Guide the student in creating a movement, if necessary.

4. Demonstrate a possible addition to the student's movement by coming very close to him and creating a repetitive movement that fits with the student's. For example, if the student is repeatedly moving an arm forward and backward, you might move your head in sync with her arm as if your head is making her arm move. Point out to the class that when adding a movement to the machine they should make it look as if they are causing a person near them to move or as if someone is causing them to move.

5. Turn on music (optional). Ask the first student to begin her repetitive movement once more. Call on other students one by one to add on to the machine. They may add themselves to any part of the machine. Encourage students to do movements at different levels—standing tall, crouching, lying on the floor, and so on. When eight to twelve students have joined the machine, allow the group's movement to continue for ten to twenty seconds, then turn off the music or signal them to stop. Repeat the activity with a new group of students.

COMMENTARY:

This activity is excellent for encouraging group cooperation. After creating several machines, you may want to use the analogy of a machine to discuss the idea of cooperation with your students—how every part of a machine, and a group, is important, and how if one part were broken the whole machine might stop working.

Although your students will probably not be completely literal in creating the type of machine they discussed in Step 2 of the Procedure, it's fun to ask them to explain how their machine works. Be sure to listen respectfully to their explanation rather than judging the accuracy or realism of their description—after all, they are the experts on their own machine!

VARIATIONS:
Rather than playing music or doing the activity in silence, ask each student to make a repetitive sound to go along with his movement. The combined rhythms of the sounds will add another layer of complexity to the machine.

To use this activity in another context, print the names of common household machines (i.e., washing machine, CD player, toaster) on cards. Give groups of four to eight students a card and ask them to illustrate, through movement, how that machine works. Give each group three minutes to prepare, then ask them to show their machine to the rest of the class.

Lesson 3
At the Post Office

A. Move and Freeze: *Moving Characters*   (15 minutes)
B. Improvisation: *At the Post Office*   (15 minutes)

A. Move and Freeze:
Moving Characters

CONTEXT:
"Let's explore the many types of people who come into a Post Office each day."

SKILLS:
Expressive use of body and movement
Understanding and expression of character

MATERIALS / PREPARATION:
- Classroom set up as a Post Office, as in Lesson 2
- Blackboard and chalk
- Hand drum, tambourine, bell, or other auditory signal

PROCEDURE:
1. Welcome the Stamp Designers back to the Post Office and tell them that they will be continuing their research by exploring the different types of people who come into a Post Office each day.

2. Ask students to name some of the people who might come into a Post Office. Encourage them to think of people of varying ages and with different occupations. Write their ideas on the blackboard. Possible examples might include:
    business person
    elderly person

mom
dad
child
truck driver
movie star, and so forth

3. Have the class read one of the words or phrases on the blackboard aloud, for example "business person." Discuss with the class why this person might come into the Post Office and what they might want to ask the Postal Worker at the counter. Also discuss the attitude or feeling the person might have as they come into the Post Office—might they be excited...in a hurry... tired...angry? Students may respond with a variety of ideas for each character. Encourage them to think beyond the stereotypes: Perhaps the business person, rather than being in a hurry, might be relaxed and cheerful because he is expecting a special package in the mail. Repeat this discussion with each of the words / phrases on the blackboard.

4. Choose a student volunteer to play a customer at the Post Office. You will play the Postal Worker. Ask the student to decide the following:
   • *Who* he or she will be. The student may select a character from the list on the board or think of a type of person that is not listed, such as a teacher or a construction worker.
   • *Why* his or her character has come into the Post Office and what question he or she will ask the Postal Worker.

5. Tell students that they will now have a chance to show how each of the people on the list might walk as they are coming into the Post Office. Explain that you will call out a description of one of the people on the list and that the students, as a group, will walk around the room as that person might walk. When you give a signal—such as beating a hand drum, striking a tambourine or ringing a bell—all students must freeze and listen for the next person to be described.

6. Call out the description of the first person on the list, for example "business person." Allow students approximately 30 seconds to walk around the room as the person you've named. As they are walking, coach students by suggesting details and asking questions about that person as in the example below:

"This business person is feeling very cheerful because she knows there is a special birthday package waiting for her. How quickly or slowly would this person walk? Would they stand tall or slouch? How would this person hold their arms? What kind of expression might this person have on her face?"

After about thirty seconds, give the signal to freeze. Repeat with each of the descriptions on the list. The following list of possible movement variations will help you coach your students as they walk:

Size of movements: big, little, medium-sized steps
Speed of movements: slow, medium, fast
Weight of movements: heavy, light
Energy of movements: smooth and graceful, sharp and jerky
Movement of specific *body parts:* How does this person move their head, arms, feet, and so forth?

COMMENTARY:

This activity gives students an initial experience in the drama skill of characterization, the idea of "becoming" a person other than oneself by taking on that person's physical and vocal attributes as well as their attitudes and motivations. This simple exercise deals mainly with the physical aspects of characterization, exploring how a person's age, occupation, and attitude may be reflected in their body.

Because they are not experienced actors, do not be surprised if your students show these characters in a very broad or even stereotyped manner by becoming, for example, a businessman who walks at twice the speed of a normal person, constantly looking at his watch, and so on. You can encourage more subtle characterizations by asking your students to attend to details: Is this person wearing tight or loose clothing and how does that affect the way they walk? What is this person worried or angry about? How large or small are her steps? Challenge the students to walk as if they *are* the business person, mother, child, and so forth rather than just showing what the person is like.

VARIATIONS:

If you wish to simplify this activity, it is possible to omit number 2 of the Procedure and have a list of characters of your own choosing decided upon in advance. Optionally, you may print this list on the blackboard.

To use this activity in the context of a literature lesson, read students a story such as "Snow White and the Seven Dwarves" by the Brothers Grimm and have the students try walking as each of the characters in the story.

B. Improvisation: *At the Post Office*

CONTEXT:
"Now let's see how the different types of people who come into a Post Office might interact with the Postal Worker at the counter."

SKILLS:
Expressive use of voice and language
Understanding and expression of character

Materials / Preparation:

• Set classroom up as a Post Office as in Lesson 2. Create a "counter" by placing one or two desks or tables at the front of the room. You will need enough space on the opposite side of the counter for five or six students to line up as customers. Designate one side of the classroom as the area where customers enter and exit the Post Office.

• The following words written on the blackboard (if you are doing this activity immediately following Activity A: "Moving Characters," simply leave your list of characters on the blackboard):

> business person
> elderly person
> mom
> dad
> child
> truck driver
> movie star

PROCEDURE:

1. Tell the Stamp Designers that they will now have a chance to experience what it is like to be a person interacting with a Postal Worker at the Post Office.

2. Have the class read one of the words or phrases on the blackboard aloud, for example "business person." Discuss with the

class why this person might come into the Post Office and what he might want to ask the Postal Worker at the counter. Also discuss the attitude or feeling the person might have as he comes into the Post Office—might they be excited...in a hurry...tired... angry? Students may respond with a variety of ideas for each character. Encourage them to think beyond the stereotypes: Perhaps the business person, rather than being in a hurry, might be relaxed and cheerful because she is expecting a special package in the mail. Repeat this discussion with each of the words / phrases on the blackboard.

3. Choose a student volunteer to play a customer at the Post Office. You will play the Postal Worker. Ask the student to decide the following:

   • *Who* he or she will be. The student may select a character from the list on the board or think of a type of person who is not listed, such as a teacher or a construction worker.

   • *Why* his or her character has come into the Post Office and what question he or she will ask the Postal Worker.

   Stand behind the counter as the Postal Worker. The volunteer will "enter" the Post Office (walk from one area of the classroom toward the counter), then stand opposite you at the postal counter.

4. Model the following procedure with the volunteer:
   a. Customer enters Post Office and stands in line at counter.
   b. Postal Worker says "May I help you?" to the customer.
   c. Customer asks Postal Worker one question.
   d. Postal Worker responds to the customer's question.
   e. Customer "exits" Post Office.

5. Tell students they will now all have a chance to play customers. Select five or six students to be the first customers. They will "enter" the Post Office and line up opposite the counter, where you are standing as the Postal Worker.

6. Repeat the improvisation demonstrated in zdtep 4. Students playing customers must each decide "who"—what character he will play and "why"—why the customer has come into the Post Office and what question he will ask the Postal Worker. Students may play a character from the list on the board or another of their own choosing. When it is her turn, each customer may ask one question. When the Postal Worker has replied to that customer, she will exit the Post Office (go to the area of the classroom that she entered from) and the next customer will step forward.

7. When everyone in the first group has had a turn to interact with the Postal Worker, ask them to return to their seats and then select five more students to enter the Post Office. Repeat the improvisation as many times as desired, ideally giving each student in the class a turn to play a customer.

COMMENTARY:

This activity, unlike Activity A: Move and Freeze: *Moving Characters*, focuses on creating characterization through voice and dialogue rather than through physical movement. Because each character's interaction with the Postal Worker will be short and structured, this simple improvisation will be relatively nonthreatening to most students.

Since the focus of this activity is on the dramatic skills of improvisation and characterization rather than on factual information about the Post Office, do not be overly concerned about whether or not the reply you give in your role as Postal Worker is "correct." Your role in this lesson is to facilitate students in creating a character with a reason to be in the scene and expressing that reason through improvised dialogue.

VARIATIONS:

After doing this activity with you in role as the Postal Worker, some students may be ready to play Postal Workers themselves. Repeat the improvisation, giving volunteers a chance to play the Postal Worker responding to customers' questions.

Do this activity in another context with students playing customers at a bank, grocery store, or library. Or, add a fanciful element by having students play talking animals who come to the Post Office.

Lesson 4
In the Field with the Mail Carriers

A. Listening / Making Sounds: *Soundscape*   (5 minutes)
B. Sound Story: *The Listening Postcard*   (8–10 minutes)
C. Drawing: *Mail Delivery Routes*   (10–15 minutes)

A. Listening / Making Sounds: *Soundscape*

CONTEXT:

"Today, we'll research Postal Workers by being out "in the field" with the Mail Carriers. This means we'll travel with them along their delivery routes to experience a typical working day of delivering mail. First, we'll imagine the kinds of sounds a Mail Carrier might hear on his delivery route."

SKILLS:
Use of the senses
Expressive use of voice

MATERIALS / PREPARATION:
Students should be seated comfortably on the floor, with enough space between them so that you can walk among them.

PROCEDURE:
1. Ask students to think of some of the different kinds of sounds a Mail Carrier might hear in the city and to say their ideas aloud when you call on them. Examples: car horn honking, baby crying in a stroller, radio playing on a boombox, and so on.

(Optional: You can modify the setting for this activity to reflect your community's environment or any other place of your choosing, such as: an industrial area, a coastline, a rural setting, and so on.)

2. Divide the class in half by drawing an imaginary line through the middle of the group. Tell students that one half of the class will make sounds while the other half listens, then they will switch roles.

3. Give students the following directions:
   - To the Sound Makers: Ask each student to decide on at least one city sound she will make. Tell them that when you tap each student on the head, he may make his sounds. Two taps on the head is the signal to stop making sounds.
   - To the Listeners: Tell them to close their eyes and listen carefully to see if they can hear all the different city sounds and imagine what each one is.

4. When the Listeners' eyes are closed and all are silent, walk around the group of Sound Makers and gently tap each student on the head, one by one. When all have been tapped, allow for 10–20 seconds of sound making and then tap each student twice until all are silent again.

5. Tell the Listeners to open their eyes. Ask them to name some of the sounds they heard when you call on them. The Sound Makers can confirm or explain the sounds that they made.

6. Switch roles and repeat the procedure.

COMMENTARY:
Encourage students to think of sounds that are not immediately obvious, such as: footsteps on the sidewalk, the sound of light rain on rooftops, a whispered conversation between two people. Encourage the Sound Makers to begin their sounds softly, thereby forcing the Listeners to concentrate more. Also, students who are self-conscious will feel safer if they are not required to make loud sounds.

VARIATIONS:

Ask students to think of some of the different kinds of sounds a Mail Carrier might hear in the countryside or other setting (such as: on an ocean island or in a factory complex) and to say their ideas aloud when you call on them. Examples: a cow mooing, a chainsaw cutting firewood, birds calling in the trees. Repeat the procedure for making and listening to sounds.

You can also have students listen to the actual sounds in your classroom or outside your building when your class is on the playground or out on a field trip. To focus on listening to actual sounds, ask students to close their eyes and be silent. Using a second hand on your watch or a kitchen timer, time the listening period for one minute. Then ask students to name the sounds they heard.

B. Sound Story:
The Listening Postcard

CONTEXT:

"I will tell you a story about the travels of a postcard. This is a Sound Story, which means you may make the sound effects."

SKILLS:

Expressive use of voice (nonverbal)
Use and development of imagination and creativity

MATERIALS / PREPARATION:

- Students will need to be facing you so that they can clearly see the sound signals you will make with your hand and arm. (You can also choose to use an object to indicate the signals, such as an arrow. Modify the sound signals as needed.)

- Photocopy the following story, "The Listening Postcard," to make it easier to hold in one hand while you signal the sounds with your other hand. An alternative method is to write out the sequence of sound cues on the board and tell the story using your own words.

PROCEDURE:

1. Tell students that this will be a Sound Story and go over the rules for the sound signals, below.

> **SOUND SIGNALS:**
> - make a fist = off
> - open hand, spread fingers = on
> - hand raises up toward ceiling = volume increases
> - hand lowers down toward floor = volume decreases

Have students practice following your signals. Demonstrate all the signals while students make these vocal sounds: 1) birds calling 2) car horns honking

2. Tell the story, using the signals as needed. Feel free to embellish or change the story as you like or make up your own. Pause at the end of each line and make the sound signals while students vocalize the appropriate sounds.

Generally, begin each sound with the "on" signal at a low volume and slowly increase the volume, allowing students to experiment with making sounds for a few moments. Then slowly decrease the volume to "off"—or allow the students to continue making the sound, softly, under your voice while you proceed with the story.

If at any time the making of sounds goes beyond your comfort level or becomes too loud for students to hear the next part of the story, simply turn the signal to "off." It's fine if students add gestures as they make sound effects, but they should remain seated.

The Listening Postcard by Pamela Gerke

I am a postcard. On one side of me is a beautiful, full-color picture of a seaside scene. My story begins in a tourist shop at the beach where I was once for sale. From my perch on the display rack by the window, I could listen to these sounds coming from outside:

ocean breezes blowing...

waves crashing on the shore...

and the sound of seagulls calling...

One day, I heard the sound of a curious little truck that played a song as it slowly drove by the shop. Can you guess what kind of truck plays a song? *(Answer: ice cream truck.)*

This ice cream truck was playing the tune of "Mary Had A Little Lamb" *(or other song of your choice).*

Then a young girl came into the shop, licking and slurping an ice cream bar.

The girl bought me and I heard the cash register ring.

The girl scribbled a note on me, addressed it, slapped on a stamp, and tossed me into a mailbox. In the bottom of the dark mailbox, it was completely and utterly silent. *(Allow for a few seconds of silence.)*

Then I heard a mail truck come, honking its horn loudly.

I was picked up and taken to a post office where I was sorted with all the other mail. As the postal workers sorted us, one worker coughed softly.

Another worker had loud hiccups.

Some of the workers were telling jokes as they sorted the mail. *(Optional: Ask students if one or two would like to tell the class a joke.)*

When the postal workers told jokes, one worker giggled in a high voice.

Another worker chuckled in a low voice.

And another worker had a very strange and unusual laugh.

After being sorted, I was put in another mail truck for delivery. As the truck took off down the street, I could hear a bicycle horn ringing, soft and high.

I couldn't see out the window of the mail truck, but we must have gone by a river for I could hear the horn of a river barge, bellowing loud and low.

Next, an ambulance drove by. (Before you make the sound, let me describe it to you:) At first, the ambulance was so far away I could barely hear the sound of the siren, it was so faint. As the ambulance got closer, the sound became louder and louder and then it faded again as the ambulance drove away.

Now you try making the sound of the ambulance siren, quietly at first (and please don't make the siren so loud that it hurts our ears!).

Then it began to rain and I could hear raindrops falling softly and lightly on the roof of the mail truck.

Suddenly, there was a flash of light and then a loud rumble of thunder!

After a while, the rain stopped. We must have driven by a school because I heard the sound of a school bell ringing for recess.

On one of our stops, I heard a dog barking.

Then I heard the mail carrier running back to the mail truck—I think she was trying to get away from the dog! I could hear her feet pounding on the sidewalk. *(Students may pound their fists on the floor.)*

She was breathing loudly and quickly from running.

On our next stop, it was my turn to be delivered. In addition to myself, the mail carrier also had a package to deliver so she rang the doorbell of the house.

When no one came to the door, the mail carrier tried knocking loudly.

Still nobody came to the door, so the mail carrier left a note, dropped me in the mail slot and left. I waited in silence. *(Allow for a few seconds of silence.)*

After awhile, the boy to whom I was addressed came home and picked me up. He looked at me for a long time as he imagined the sounds of my postcard picture:

ocean breezes blowing...

waves crashing on the shore...

and the sound of seagulls calling...

The boy looked at my beautiful picture and he gave a big sigh.

The End

COMMENTARY:

Sound Stories encourage expressive use of the voice while actively engaging the imagination. Do not be concerned at first if the students' sounds are tentative or inaccurate. It's best if you do not demonstrate the sounds yourself or tell students how to make them, so that they can make their own discoveries. Use of the sound signals will keep you in control of the activity.

Just as in Move and Freeze activities you employ the dramatic contrast of movement and stillness, here you employ the contrast of sound and silence. These contrasts, as well as light and darkness, are also known as "the spectra of theater" and can be used in classroom drama to focus attention and to heighten dramatic tension. This story also makes use of the sound contrasts of loud/quiet (or soft) and high/low, requiring students to use their voices expressively in a wide range of both volume and pitch.

VARIATIONS:

Sounds can be made with parts of the body other than voices, such as by clapping hands or pounding the floor. You could also use percussion and other musical instruments. First, decide with the class which instrument will play which sound in the story; for example, rain sticks for ocean waves and raindrops; drums for the river barge horn, thunder and pounding feet; handbells for the truck, barge and bicycle horns for the doorbell; wood sticks for the door knocking; kazoos for the ice cream truck, the laughing of the postal workers and the siren. All other sounds will be made vocally.

Sound Stories can also be combined with movement as students mime the actions of the stories while making the appropriate sounds; or, half the group makes the sounds while the other half does the movement.

Another variation is to give students the opportunity to "conduct" the sound effects. Have students practice making the Sound Signals with their hands and arms. Then, with students standing in a row or in a circle, read "The Listening Postcard" and have each student, one at a time, conduct one or more of the sound cues.

C. Drawing: *Mail Delivery Routes*

This activity adds a visual art component to the dramatic context and can be used as part of a movement and pantomime activity.

CONTEXT:
"A Mail Carrier must have a map in order to know where to go on his delivery route."

SKILLS:
Drawing and designing
Use and development of imagination and creativity

MATERIALS / PREPARATION:
- Blank paper and pencils, markers or crayons for all students
- Blackboard and chalk

PROCEDURE:
1. Tell students that they will each draw a map of a mail delivery route in an imaginary neighborhood. Ask students for suggestions of the kinds of places that might be found in such a neighborhood, for example: various buildings (houses, stores, a library, a community center), parks, parking lots, a waterfront, streets, highways, and so forth.

    Tell students that they must draw at least three neighborhood places on their maps and connect them together with a line that represents the Mail Carrier's delivery route.

    Demonstrate by drawing a simple map on the blackboard. Show students that they can draw simple symbols to represent each place. For example, you might draw a box to indicate a house, a flag to indicate the post office and a star to indicate the police station. Draw a line between these three symbols to show the mail delivery route.

    When you feel sure students understand the assignment, erase your sample map so that they don't think this is the "correct" map and they will not be tempted to simply copy it.

2. Give each student blank paper and pencils, markers, or crayons. Allow approximately 10–15 minutes for students to draw their delivery maps as you circulate among them. (If needed, you can give students time to complete this activity later.)

VARIATIONS:

You can use these student-generated maps as a part of a movement and pantomime activity. Students can imagine that your classroom is the neighborhood of their imaginary maps and, with maps in hand, travel around the room, pantomiming delivering mail to the various places on their own maps. Begin by asking each student to choose one place in your classroom to be the starting point for their own mail delivery route. Each student can decide which of the places on his own map this starting point corresponds to.

For example, one student might choose to begin at the doorway that she has decided represents the "clothing store" on her map, while another student might choose his own desk as his starting point, which he has decided is the "city pool" on his map. At your signal, students travel from place to place as if they are traveling the route indicated on their maps, while they pantomime and improvise dialogue as Mail Carriers. It's not crucial that students make precise correspondences between their maps and the layout of your class-room.

You can also use these maps to inspire a dance/movement activity. Students travel from place to place as in the activity described above but at each place (symbol) on their "route" they stop, make an interesting shape with their bodies and hold it for a few seconds, then continue to the next place. Another variation is to also have students travel from place to place in some way other than walking such as skipping, hopping, crawling, tiptoeing, and so on. For example, a student might skip to her first place (the fire station on her map), stop and curl into a ball, hold that shape for a few seconds, then hop to their second place (the house on her map), stop and make a shape like the letter X, hold that shape for a few seconds, then tiptoe to their next place, and so forth.

Lesson 5
Home Visit

A. Rhythm Game: *Pass the Salt*   (10 minutes)
B. Tableaux: *Family Photo Album*   (20 minutes)

A. Rhythm Game: *Pass the Salt*

Thanks to Clayton Miller for this idea
adapted from Dalcroze Eurythmics.

CONTEXT:
"We arrive at a Postal Worker's home at dinner time and we're asked to join his family for dinner."

SKILLS:
Ability to focus attention
Awareness and control of body (combined with rhythm)

MATERIALS / PREPARATION:
You will need sufficient space for the entire class to comfortably stand in a circle.

PROCEDURE:
1. Have students stand with you in a circle. Tell them that they have been invited to join the Postal Worker and his family at the dinner table and will play a game called "Pass the Salt."

2. Teach students the following chant, spoken in rhythm:

Pass the Salt

Pass, pass, pass the salt, pass the bread and cheese.

Pass, pass, pass the salt, pass the pep - per, please!

(The mark at the end of each line is called a "rest" which means it is a silent beat.)

3. Now teach students the following movements:

- Students hold their right hand palm-side up and their left hand palm-side down.

- While all speak the chant (slowly at first) you, the teacher, begin by tapping your left hand on the upturned palm of the person to your left (their right hand). That person then taps their left hand on the upturned palm of the person to their left, and so forth around the circle (clockwise).

- Each tap will be on one beat of the chant, including the "rests." The idea is to keep the beat steady.

- Begin slowly and maintain a steady tempo. When students have mastered the pattern at a slow tempo, stop the game and restart it at a slightly faster tempo.

4. Add variations as desired:

- Change the direction of the "passing" movements to counter-clockwise (going to the right).

- Randomly, at the "rests," the teacher calls out, "Beep!" When students hear this signal, they must reverse the direction of the movements, i.e., change the movements from going to the left to going to the right (or vice versa), while keeping the beat steady.

- Whenever the teacher calls out, "Beep!" students reverse the direction of the palm-tapping movements, as for Variation B, above. This time, instead of saying the chant, students count aloud for 4 beats: "1-2-3-4," while continuing to do the palm-tapping movements. After the count of 4, students resume saying the chant while continuing to do the palm-tapping movements.

- For extra challenges: At the "Beep!" signal, students reverse the direction of their movements, but this time they must count to 8 (or another number higher than 4) before resuming saying the chant (all the while continuing to do the palm-tapping movements). For a bonus challenge: When students resume speaking the chant, they must once again reverse the direction of the "passing" movements.

COMMENTARY:
This game is adapted from a Dalcroze Eurythmics activity. Named after Emile Jaques-Dalcroze (1865–1950), the Swiss musician and educator who developed this approach, Dalcroze Eurythmics is a method for teaching music through rhythmic movement, eartraining, and improvisation. These activities are applicable to drama education as well for they aid in the development of attention, concentration, memory, coordination, self-control, kinesthetic awareness and coordination, and personal expressiveness.

VARIATIONS:
Repeat this game throughout the school year and as students become more skillful, you can increase the challenges with suggested variations (Procedure, Step 4). Here are some other variations: At the "Beep!" signal, students reverse the direction of passing *and* keep silent while they continue silently reciting the chant in their minds. When they hear the next "Beep!" students resume speaking the chant aloud. Pass an object, such as a ball, around the circle. Have students make up their own chants with the same meter as "Pass the Salt."

B. Tableaux: *Family Photo Album*

CONTEXT:
"Today we'll visit the homes of Post Office workers in order to expe-rience their family lives as part of our stamp design research. The family you are visiting would like to show you their Family Photo Album."

SKILLS:
Understanding and expression of character and setting
Collaboration and negotiation with others

MATERIALS / PREPARATION:
- (Optional) A family photo album to show students
- Blackboard and chalk

PROCEDURE:
1. If you have a family photo album, show the students several of the photos. Ask students, "What are some things that families do together?" Allow as many students as wish to respond, listening respectfully to all answers. Write each of their answers on the blackboard. Possible responses might include eating dinner, playing at the beach, working in the yard, playing a game, etc.

2. Tell students that they will now be creating some "photographs"—frozen pictures, which are also called "tableaux"—with their bodies. These photographs will depict the family lives of some Postal Workers. Select a group of five or six students to come to the front of the room to create the first tableau.

3. Select a family activity from the list generated by the students in Step 1, either by choosing one of the activities yourself or having the students in the performing group quickly decide which activity they would like to represent. Tell the group that they will be creating a frozen picture or tableau of a family doing that activity.

For example, if the activity chosen is "playing at the beach," the group will create their own tableau of a family at the beach.

4. Without allowing the rest of the class to hear, assign each member of the group a family member to play (mother, father, sister, grandmother, uncle, and so on). Let individual performers decide what their family member would be doing in the scene. In the example, "playing at the beach": One student might be the father swimming with his daughter (another student), two students might play the grandfather and grandmother eating lunch, and another student might be their grandson digging in the sand. Give the group a minute or two to discuss and organize their tableau, reminding them that they need to create a scene without movement, like a still photograph.

5. When the group has organized their tableau, explain the following procedure:
   • You will count aloud "1...2...3" as the group gets into position for their photograph.
   • You will say "Freeze," at which time the group will hold their positions for 5 seconds while the rest of the class watches.
   • You will clap your hands or say "Unfreeze," at which time the group will unfreeze their photograph.
   • The rest of the class may now guess what family roles were represented in the scene and what each family member was doing. The performing group may also clarify and explain what was happening in their photograph, after which they will sit down.
   • You will select a new group and repeat the procedure, giving each student a chance to perform.

6. Do the procedure described above. Repeat the procedure until each student in the class has had a chance to participate, choosing additional family activities from the list generated in Step 1. If desired, allow each group the option of coming up with their own idea for a family photo scene.

7. After all students have had a turn to participate in a family photograph tableau, ask the first group to come forward and make their tableau again. Tell them that you would now like to hear what each family member is thinking. Explain that when you tap someone on the shoulder, that person will remain frozen but will speak aloud what their character in the photograph is thinking. For example, the character might say a sentence about what she is seeing, hearing, smelling, touching, or tasting, such as: "This water is really cold!" or "I hear seagulls in the distance." They might also say something about another person in the photograph, such as: "I wish my brother would stop splashing me," or "I'm glad Grandma came to the beach with us today."

8. Tap one student in the frozen tableau on the shoulder and allow him a moment to speak as his character in the photograph. If necessary, coach students by asking what they are experiencing with their senses, or what they are thinking about another family member in the photograph. After each student speaks her thoughts, she resumes a frozen position. Allow each student in the group an opportunity to speak. When finished, clap your hands as a signal for the group to unfreeze. Ask the group to be seated, then repeat this procedure with the remaining groups.

COMMENTARY:

This activity is a relatively nonthreatening step toward having students improvise scenes based on real-life situations. Because they remain frozen in position and do not speak to one another, students do not yet need to create action and dialogue. They must, however, decide on actions appropriate to the setting and imagine what their characters in the scene might be thinking.

Steps 7 and 8 of this activity introduce students to the idea of "inner dialogue," the concept that each character in a play must actually think thoughts related to what is happening in the scene. The practice of maintaining inner dialogue helps keep actors focused on what is actually happening in the scene rather than on how they are appearing to the audience.

It is important to be aware that children today come from a diverse range of family backgrounds. Many of your students may live with just one parent, with another relative such as a grandparent or aunt, or an unrelated guardian. Children of gay couples may have two mothers or two fathers. One of the goals of this second- and third-grade drama curriculum is to make students aware of the differences and similarities between families. With this in mind, be sure to respect any choices your students make in their portrayal of family groups and encourage them to be sensitive to each other with regard to this issue.

VARIATIONS:

To simplify this lesson, eliminate Procedures 7 and 8 and have each group create a frozen tableau without inner dialogue. You may also present Procedures 7 and 8 as a separate activity in another class session.

Integrate the study of family life in different cultures by reading stories or displaying photographs that portray life in a Japanese family, a Native American Family, an African family, and so forth. After discussing the similarities and differences in family activities between cultures, have students create tableaux showing family life in cultures other than their own.

Show the class photographs from magazines or reproductions of paintings depicting people in various situations. Call on students to tell you what each person in a photograph or painting might be thinking.

Lesson 6
More Research

A. Mirroring: *Copycat*   (10 minutes)

B. Story Creation: *Ring, Book, and Teacup*   (10–15 minutes)

A. Mirroring: *Copycat*

CONTEXT:

"As we are doing our stamp design research, we must observe the actions of the Postal Workers carefully, so that we can copy them accurately for our stamp designs."

SKILLS:

Use and development of powers of observation and awareness of details

Awareness and control of body parts

MATERIALS / PREPARATION:

- You will need enough space for students to move in Self Space freely, without touching others, and so that they can see you.
- (Optional) CD or tape player and a CD or tape of soft, peaceful instrumental music

PROCEDURE:

1. Make sure you are standing in a position in which you can be easily seen by all students. Tell students that their job is to watch you closely and to copy your movements as accurately as possible. Turn on the music (optional).

2. Facing your students and staying in one place, begin to do slow, simple movements with your body. For example, stretch you arms in different directions, nod or circle your head, shrug your shoulders, twist from side to side. Students move at the same time as you, copying your movements as in a mirror image.

Continue your movements for 1–2 minutes, then end by freezing in a shape. (Turn off the music.)

3. Divide your class into pairs and designate one student in each pair as "leader." Tell students that each pair will now practice "mirroring": Partners face each other and the "leaders" do simple movements that their partner tries to copy exactly. Turn on the music (optional) while students practice mirroring for 1–2 minutes.

4. Switch leaders in each pair and give students another 1–2 minutes to practice mirroring.

COMMENTARY:
Mirroring is an excellent beginning drama exercise in concentration, body awareness, and attention to detail. You do not need to be an experienced dancer to lead a mirroring exercise: Simply think about moving one body part at a time. Keep your movements slow and simple so that they can be easily imitated by students. Soothing background music will help alleviate self-consciousness for both you and your students.

VARIATIONS:
As your students build skill in movement, you may want to give volunteers turns to lead the class in mirroring. You can also use mirroring as a regular activity whenever you want to focus the attention of your students. It's a great way to give restless bodies an energy boost after a period of sitting. You can also do the mirroring activity while students are seated at their desks.

Another variation is to have pairs of students mirror in front of the class, one pair at a time, while the rest of the class watches and tries to guess which student is the leader and which is the follower.

B. Story Creation:
Ring, Book, and Teacup

CONTEXT:
"For our research on families for our stamp designs, we'll examine some objects that might be kept within a family for a long time, "passed down" from one generation to the next. Let's make up some stories about these objects."

SKILLS:
Collaboration and negotiation with others
Story creation

MATERIALS / PREPARATION:
- A ring, an old book, and a fancy or delicate teacup
- Begin by having students sit in a circle on the floor, facing each other.

PROCEDURE:
1. Tell students that sometimes certain objects are kept within families for several generations. Ask students to share with the class if they know of any objects that have been "passed down," or inherited, within their own families, such as furniture, china, jewelry, clothing.

2. Show students the ring and pass it around the circle for all to inspect. Ask students to imagine that it is a ring that has been in a family for many generations. Tell them that together, your class will make up a story about the ring and the family it belongs to. When all students have inspected the ring, place it in the center of the circle.

3. Guide students in creating a story together: Students may spontaneously contribute their ideas as you help them shape a story by asking questions, making statements, and continually reiterating

the story as it progresses. The story can be either "true to life" or a fantasy. The only "given" is that the ring has been passed down in the same family for many generations. The following is a suggested procedure for group story creation about "the ring":

- Ask students to imagine how the ring first came to this family long ago, for example:

  "Did someone buy the ring or did they make it themselves? Who was that person? Where did they live? What was that person's purpose in buying or making this ring? Was the ring their own or a gift for someone else?"

- As the story develops, continue to ask questions as needed to help motivate and structure the story, for example:

  "Is there anything special about this ring?"

  "I wonder if this ring has been involved in an adventure..."

  "What happened first in the story of the ring? What happened next?"

- In a continuing narration, clarify suggested ideas and incorporate them into the story line as it develops, recapping events as needed; for example:

  "So, after the woman bought the ring at a bazaar, she discovered it was magical. She said the magic words—'tasha-washa-pum'—and flew to Korea. There, she married a fireman and they had three children. What happened to the ring after that?" (and so forth)

- If needed, remind students that the ring has been kept in the same family through many generation by saying such things as:

  "Why did the people in the story keep the ring in their family instead of selling it?"

  "Which family member did the person give the ring to next?"

You may have to politely discard any suggested ideas that con-tradict other ideas that have already been incorporated into the story. You will have to use your best judgment in choosing which ideas to include and which to discard without making any students feel slighted.

The story need not be long, have a well-developed plot, or be factually accurate. This is an activity in imagination and collaboration, and you can allow ideas to flow. At the same time, be aware of creating a beginning, middle, and end of your story.

4. Repeat the procedure to create a story about the book or the teacup.

COMMENTARY:

There is great value for all artists in what in writing is called "fluency"; that is, "being capable of flowing." In this lesson, it is the imagination that can flow unfettered, much as it does in "brainstorming." That's why we suggest that you allow students to spontaneously speak their ideas out loud, rather than having them raise their hands or take turns around the circle. Creativity is not always orderly and ideas don't appear only when called upon. If you can allow for a little bit of excited energy, your class will be able to experience fluency in story creating.

The danger, of course, is that the most outspoken, aggressive students will dominate the story creation. Encourage all students to contribute and make sure you are incorporating everyone's ideas, even if you feel you can manage this activity better by having students raise their hands. If you choose to have students take turns around the circle, you can allow students to say, "Pass."

This activity foreshadows the role drama to come in Part III: "The Mystery Letter," as the ring and the book will be mentioned in the Letter. In this lesson, students generate ideas about the objects as related to families in order to lay some groundwork for the drama they will create in Part III.

Indirectly, the ring, book, and teacup are used here as symbols of family connections. Use of symbols can generate shared meaning among your students—that is, a collective understanding of the significance of those symbols as they relate to students' own lives and experiences. Drama in the classroom offers a unique opportunity for students to relate to the universal human experience. For example, the passing down of objects represents the continuity of families over many generations. Symbols may offer individual meaning to students as well. For example, for one student a ring may make her sad about her parents' divorce; for another student a fancy ring may symbolize his family's wealth; for another, a ring reminds her of her great grandfather who used to wear a special ring.

VARIATIONS:

Instead of having students spontaneously contribute ideas aloud, you can ask students to raise their hands to share their ideas when you call upon them. Or, you can go around the circle taking turns making up the story. (Please see Commentary.)

You can use any kind of object to stimulate an original story with your class, including objects that relate to other subjects your class is studying. For example, if you were preparing for a field trip to your local natural history museum you could use a replica of a dinosaur skull as your story stimulus. Or, if your class was going to meet with a visual art specialist you could stimulate a story with a painting or sculpture.

PART III

THE MYSTERY LETTER

Special thanks to Susan Anderson
for her help in developing this section.

In the next four lessons you and your students will embark on a creative experience that we refer to as a "spontaneous role drama." It is not entirely spontaneous, however, as students will be making decisions at various points along the way in order to create their own drama. In this way, they act as playwrights and directors as well as participants in the action. This experience can be challenging for the teacher, as it is literally impossible to predict exactly what will happen. But for this very reason a role drama carries a huge amount of potential for learning and growth for everyone involved.

Spontaneous role drama works on a very different model from most educational strategies. Most learning experiences are structured in advance by the teacher, whose plans are then carried out by the students. In spontaneous role drama teacher and students work together to structure an experience at the same time they are engaging in it. Here, the teacher is as much of a participant as the students, and the students have as much say over what will happen as the teacher.

In spite of the apparent risk of such an open-ended activity, the teacher need never fear losing her place as the authority in the classroom. Although the students are involved in the decision making in a spontaneous role drama, the teacher always has ultimate control of class management and safety. The following are several guidelines to help you make this role drama a successful and fruitful experience for you and your students.

Facilitate Decision Making

Allow your students an opportunity to be involved in appropriate decision making. In initial drama experiences it is best to ask students to choose between a small number of alternatives ("Shall the letter be from Europe or from Africa?") rather than giving them an open-ended choice ("Where shall the letter be from?"). You can also progressively narrow down choices: After a group has made the choice to have the letter be from Europe rather than from Africa, their next choice can be which country in Europe it was mailed from.

It is quite common for children to make choices that seem inappropriate ("Let's have the Letter Writer and Recipient be killed!"). Your job, as a teacher, is to make them aware of the implications of such choices to their drama rather than to reject their decisions or moralize. For example, when faced with the comment above you might say, "If they were both killed, would there still be a reason to solve this case?" In this way you let your students know that their ideas are being heard and considered, but that every idea carries with it a consequence that they must be prepared to accept.

In a role drama some decision making can be done by voting while other decisions are best made by consensus. There will also be situations in which it is fine for you, as teacher, to make a decision yourself in order to keep the momentum of the drama going. See Chapter 4 "Managing Drama Activities in the Classroom," section on "Facilitating Group Decision Making" for a complete discussion of when it is appropriate to use each of the decision-making processes mentioned above.

Slow the Pace

Remember that your major goal in a spontaneous role drama is to deepen your students' belief in an imaginary situation and to provide them with the opportunity to have an internal connection to the subject matter they are engaged in—not to create an exciting story with a well-constructed plot line. Because of their experiences with stories, TV, and films, your students may very well want to rush to create a "climax." Slow them down, hold them back, keep them focused on the physical tasks that need to be done in their imaginary world. When the pace of the drama is slowed, children are more available for feeling and reflection about what they are doing. If an exciting event does end up taking place, it will be much more satisfying if the students have been challenged to make the setting, objects, and situation of the drama real for themselves. The following are some techniques that may be used when you wish to slow the pace:

- Freeze the physical action and ask a reflective question.

- Have the students perform their physical actions in slow motion.

- Restrain the students from moving the story line forward prematurely by asking them to engage fully in a repetitive physical task within the drama.

- Delay and build anticipation about the arrival of a character or event by asking the students to form visual images of what it might look like. (For example, "What do you imagine might be in the letter?")

Provide Opportunities for Reflection

One of the most important reasons for doing a spontaneous role drama with your students is for the reflection on oneself and one's relationship to the world that such an experience provides. Rather than simply "doing" a drama, students need a chance to think about what they are experiencing and feeling. In asking a reflective question you are encouraging, rather than demanding, that students share their thoughts and feelings. Avoid asking questions that begin with the word "why," because such questions may cause students to become defensive, thinking that they are being asked to justify themselves. Asking questions that may simply be answered "yes" or "no" rarely lead to real reflection. The best reflective questions are concrete, and relate directly to what the student is experiencing in the drama: "What are you thinking about as we wait for the Writer to arrive at the Post Office?" Reflection can also be encouraged through statements of observation about elements of the drama: "I wonder how the Writer feels about this reunion?" (Also see sections on "Asking Questions" and "Facilitating Reflection" in Chapter 2, "The Classroom Teacher as Drama Instructor.")

Structure of The Mystery Letter

Because of the unpredictable nature of spontaneous role drama, we have provided you with both an outline for procedure, including possible alternatives (Lessons 7–10), and a scripted example (see "The Mystery Letter: An Example") to show how the lesson might progress with a group of second- or third-graders. Please do not regard the example as a set script to work from or you will deprive your students of the opportunity to make decisions about their own drama.

We have outlined "The Mystery Letter" to be completed in four periods of approximately 30–45 minutes each. For the sake of building and maintaining momentum with this role drama, we suggest that you do "The Mystery Letter" lessons on consecutive days or nearly consecutive days, rather than having a break of several days between each drama session.

Lesson 7
The Mystery Letter, Part 1

Preparation: *The Envelope*   (10–15 minutes)
The Designers Become Postal Detectives   (25–40 minutes)

INTRODUCTION

In the first part of this lesson students are asked to make some decisions regarding the information on the envelope of the Mystery Letter: the country of its origin and the names of both the letter writer and the family member to whom it is addressed. In the second part of this lesson students, in role as the Stamp Designers, are approached by a Post Office Official (yourself or another adult) for their help in solving this case. They are "sworn in" as Post Office detectives and then read the letter and begin to examine it for clues to help them find the intended recipient.

Preparation: *The Envelope*

Do this activity either earlier in the day or a full day before you begin the role drama that follows.

PROCEDURE:

1. Tell students (as their teacher, not in role as the Design Company Secretary) that today an unexpected turn of events will occur: A Post Office Official will approach the Stamp Designers for their help in solving the case of a "Mystery Letter." The Post Office is unable to deliver this letter because part of the address is smudged. The Stamp Designers will be asked to become temporary detectives for the postal service.

2. Take a few moments for your class to discuss this idea, asking students questions and suggesting possible implications such as:

"If we get involved with this case, we'll have to do some detective

work. We're stamp designers—are we capable of being detectives as well?"

"What if there is some kind of problem or special challenge involved with this Mystery Letter—are we still willing to attempt to solve this case?"

"Will our getting involved in this case add to our research on postal workers? Or will it take too much time away from our stamp-design research?"

3. After your class has discussed the idea of becoming temporary postal detectives and working on the case of the Mystery Letter, they must decide some of the details about the Mystery Letter's envelope. You will now facilitate group decisions about following information:

- the country from which the letter was mailed

- the names of both the person who mailed the letter ("The Writer") and the person to whom it is addressed ("The Recipient")

TO DECIDE THE COUNTRY:

When making this group decision, it is expedient to offer students a limited number of choices and then vote by majority rule. (If desired, you can allow more time for discussion about various countries and for arriving at a group consensus.) The following is a suggested method for quickly deciding which country the Mystery Letter comes from:

- Offer students a choice between two continents, for example: "Will the letter be from Europe or from Africa?" Take a vote if needed.

- Ask for suggestions of 6–8 specific countries in that chosen continent and write students' suggestions on the blackboard.

- Take a vote to select one country.

TO DECIDE THE NAMES OF BOTH
THE WRITER AND THE RECIPIENT:

The Letter should be:

- from one person to another (rather than to or from a company or organization)

- from one family member to another; therefore, the two people should have the same last name

At this point, you can simply inform students as to whether the Writer and Recipient are female or male. (You can, of course, vote on this decision as well, but in order to avoid a girls-against-boys battle, we recommend you make this decision yourself.)

Ask students if they know of any typical names of people who live in the country they've chosen. Either list ideas on the board and take a vote, or simply accept the first good idea. For example, "Patrick is a good Irish name—the Writer will be named Patrick." Give the Writer and Recipient a last name as well (the same for each).

The Designers Become Postal Detectives

You may need to clarify for students that the premise and procedures of this scene and the accompanying "oath" are entirely fictitious and are in no way based on the actual process for tracing letters through the U.S. Postal System.

CONTEXT:
"After doing research on Postal Workers, the Stamp Designers return to their studio to begin designing postage stamps. A Post Office Official approaches the Designers for help in solving the case of where to deliver a "Mystery Letter."

SKILLS:
Commitment to believing in imaginary situations
Collaboration

MATERIALS / PREPARATION:
- The Letter: On a sheet of paper handwrite the following letter, filling in the information pertinent to your own class's drama (underlined in this sample). The alphabet letters that are large and in bold are a "secret code" that reads "Ma's will" (Please see Commentary for information about the implications embodied in this letter.)

You may also choose to rewrite the letter in your own words as long as it includes:

- an element of mystery about what happened between the Writer and Recipient

- ambiguity about the details (to give students the opportunity to create their own drama)
- a sense of urgency about the Writer and Recipient finding each other.

You may also choose to write your own secret code that challenges your students' abilities and that has implications for some type of familial problem or relationship.

Dear (name of the Letter Recipient),

I can't get out of **M**y mind what happened the last time we were together...

Against all odds, I'm coming to (name of the city where your school is located) on (the date you plan to do Lesson 10).

Let**'S** meet at the post office. *Please!!!*

We *must* take care of this terrible problem—**I**'m afraid of what could happen!

I will bring the ring. I hope to heaven you sti**LL** have the book.

Love,
(name of Letter Writer)

- In order for all of your students to be able to see the letter at the same time, you will also need to do one of the following:

  - Make a copy of the letter on a plastic transparency sheet for an overhead projector

  - Or, make a second copy of the letter on butcher paper in large print. (In the case of the latter, you will tape the butcher-paper copy to the wall at the appropriate time.)

- You will need an overhead projector and screen, if available. (If using the butcher-paper copy of the letter instead, you will need tape.)

- The Envelope: (Place the letter in the envelope and seal it.)

---

name of Letter Writer   postage stamp
fictitious address in the   (drawing)
country your class has chosen

           Name of Letter Recipient
           (smudged address)
           city, state and zip code of your school
URGENT!

- Paper and pencils, one for each student

- As needed, set up your classroom as the Designer's studio (see "Starting Out").

- Blackboard and chalk

- It may be best to have another adult play the role of the Post Office Official, as you will also be in role as the Designer's Secretary (although it's fine if you play both roles). Brief your guest beforehand about the role of the Official (see Commentary).

  The Official will need to be carrying the Mystery Letter and either have a good understanding of what the Official will say or carry a photocopy of the suggested "script" (steps 3–6, below).

PROCEDURE:

1. Invite your students to "begin a moment in the life of the Designers." The Designers are in their studio, working on drawing stamp designs. Ask students, "Are we ready to begin? What tasks are we doing in the studio when the Post Office Official arrives?"

   This is an opportunity for your students to spend some time in role as the Designers, doing the work of designing stamps based on their research of Post Office workers. Pass out pencils and paper and, in role as their Secretary, encourage students to recall the activities they did in Lessons 1–6, while reminding them of the requirements of the stamp design competition (see "Starting Out").

After students have spent about 10–15 minutes drawing stamp designs, ask your adult guest to enter in role as the Post Office Official. (If you yourself will be in this role, exit the room briefly and re-enter as the Official.)

3. The Post Office Official arrives and says the following (or paraphrase in your own words):

"Hello, I am (make up a name), the head of our city's Post Office. We have recently received a letter at the Post Office that we are unable to deliver because the address is smudged. This letter is marked "Urgent!" (Pause to pass the envelope around for students to examine.)

"At the Post Office we're so overworked right now that no one has time to find out where this letter should be delivered. I realize your work is in stamp design, but since you have been working so closely with us for the last few weeks, you know a lot about the work of the Post Office as well.

We need your help. I've come to ask you to become detectives for the postal service so that you can help us solve the case of where to deliver this "Mystery Letter." Can I count on your assistance? Any questions?" (The Official answers questions.)

4. The Designers must now be "sworn in" as temporary detectives for the Post Office and take an "oath of confidentiality." The Official (or you, the teacher) should explain to students what this means and not proceed until they understand. You can say something like:

"As Detectives you will be allowed to open the letter and read it in order to get information to help you figure out where to deliver it. When you take this oath, you are agreeing that you will not tell anyone else what's in the letter."

5. The Official now instructs the Designers to stand either in front of their desks or in a circle, facing the Official. The Designers must hold up their right hands while the Official recites the following (or paraphrase in your own words):

"Do you, members of the (name of your stamp-design company), swear to keep secret what is in any letter you read as U.S. Postal detectives? I will come to each of you in turn and you each must look me in the eye and say, 'Yes, I do.'"

(The Official does so. Each student says, "Yes, I do.")

"By the power invested in me by the U.S. Postmaster General, I hereby declare you, members of (name of your stamp-design company), to be Detectives of the U.S. Postal System."

6. The Official shakes students' hands and congratulates them, gives the Mystery Letter to one of the Designers, and exits.

7. After you (or a student) opens the Letter, tell the Designers that you will make a copy for the overhead projector so that everyone can read it together. Pretend to do so (such as by putting the letter in your desk drawer, making a copy machine sound, then pulling the plastic transparency copy out of that same drawer). Show the Letter on the overhead projector. (If you don't have access to an overhead projector, post your large, butcher-paper copy of the letter on the wall at this time.)

8. With your class, read the letter aloud. Students will most likely notice that some of the alphabet letters are larger and will try to figure out why this is so. This will lead them to wonder what the hidden message is, and how "Ma's will" could be connected to the other contents of the letter. At this point they may want to

share what they know about wills. Allow students to spontaneously speak their ideas aloud about the Letter, as time permits.

Ask students to think about the Mystery Letter before the next drama lesson and to see what clues about the Writer and Recipient they can gather from it.

COMMENTARY:

In this lesson, the drama curriculum "changes gears" and moves from a focus on developing drama skills—via the context of the Designers' research on Postal Workers—to the creation of the students' own spontaneous role drama. This drama is intended to be a further exploration of the theme of family and community. As Postal Detectives, students are in role as members of their community's postal service while actively engaging in a drama about two family members who have became separated and who urgently need to reunite. Students make initial decisions about the drama, and in doing so take ownership of their experience, building interest and belief in the imaginary situation. At the same time they are collaborating to create a story ("playwriting").

This letter has been designed to foreshadow possibilities for the role drama to come. The Letter mentions a ring, a book (two of the items from Lesson 6), and "Ma's will" in order to suggest a point of origin for the plot of the drama and to imply a story about a family. The wording of the Letter is intended to imply a sense of urgency and a time constraint (the Letter is "urgent" and the Writer will appear on a certain day).

Foreshadowing is a basic element of drama and literature that creates dramatic tension. Constraints—limits on time, place, or action—are devices used as a foundation for building dramatic tension. Another kind of tension is also created here in the form of anticipation: After students have preplanned some of the information on the envelope, they will be invested in the planning of the Mystery Letter drama and will anticipate seeing what happens when the Post Office Official arrives, as well as finding out what the Letter contains.

The ceremony for inducting the Designers as Postal Detectives, including the oath of confidentiality, is included as a "ritual of commitment." Rituals are employed in role drama to help build students' belief in and commitment to the drama. With the act of raising their right hands, looking the Official in the eye and saying, "Yes, I will," each student affirms their agreement to continued investment in the drama. The formality of the oath "upgrades" the scene and lends a feeling of realism.

If any students are reluctant to go along with the drama, you can always stop the work and, as their teacher, encourage them to believe in some part of it. For example, if a student says, "That's not a real Post Office Official—that's my mother!" you might say, "Of course it's your mother, we all know that. But are you willing to believe for now that she's a Postal Official?" It's important to take the time to engage all your students in their commitment to proceeding with the drama. It is helpful to involve students with real tasks, such as drawing stamp design ideas and deciphering the letter's secret code.

The appearance of another adult in role as the Post Office Official is exciting for your students and can contribute to building belief in the drama. Give your guest the information they will need to impart to the Designers (a photocopy of steps 3–6 of the Procedure) and they can use this as a script or paraphrase it in their own words. It's important that your guest understand that she is not to "act," to entertain, or perform. Your guest's role is to lend a realistic tone to this moment and to help move the action of the drama to the next stage. The Post Office Official should convey the attitude of someone who has the power to induct the Designers as Postal Detectives.

Lesson 8
The Mystery Letter, Part 2

*What Happened the Last Time the
Writer and Recipient Were Together* (30–45 minutes)

In this lesson, students create the story of the last time the Mystery Letter Writer and Recipient were together. Working in pairs and trios, students develop story ideas and improvise this moment in the lives of the two people. The pairs and trios then share their ideas with the rest of the class. (Note: We refer to the two family members of the Mystery Letter as "The Writer and Recipient" but from now on, substitute the names you have decided upon for the two people.)

What Happened the Last Time the Writer and Recipient Were Together

CONTEXT:
"As Postal Detectives, we must look for clues to help us solve this case. We will piece the clues together to create a story of what might have happened the last time the two people in the Mystery Letter were together."

SKILLS:
Story creation / playwriting
Artistic collaboration

MATERIALS / PREPARATION:
   Blackboard and chalk

PROCEDURE:
   1. Tell students that in order to solve the case of the Mystery Letter they must first see what clues they can find in the Letter itself.

Reread the Letter aloud. Now brainstorm with students all that they know about the Writer and Recipient. Ask questions and make statements encouraging students to consider what clues there may be regarding the story behind the Letter. For example:

> *"I wonder what could have happened the last time these two people were together."*

> *"I'm curious what 'Ma's will' is all about."*

> *"What do you think 'the ring' and 'the book' have to do with the hidden message?"*

> *"I wonder what the 'terrible problem' could be...?"*

Write students' ideas on the board. You list might include:

- The names of the Writer and Recipient are: _____

- The letter was sent from:_____

- Some "problem" happened the last time they were together

- The Writer will be here at the post office on:_____

- The Writer has a ring and the Recipient has a book.

- There is a hidden message about their mother's will.

2. Inform students that they will use some or all of these clues to imagine the moment of "The last time the letter Writer and Recipient were together." Explain that there are three things students must decide when they create the story. Write the following on the blackboard: *Who, What, Where.* Ask students to imagine:

> *Who* are the two people and how are they related to each other?
> *What* happened the last time they were together?
> *Where* were they at that time?

3. Tell students they will now work in pairs or trios. Explain that each pair or trio will:

- Make up a story about the last time the Writer and Recipient were together. They must decide the "Who, What, Where" for their story using some of the clues from the Mystery Letter.

- Decide who will take which role (the Writer, the Recipient, and if desired, other people, such as their mother).

- Experiment with improvising a story. Groups can stop and start over as often as they like, trying out different ideas or refining the ones they already have. (See "The Mystery Letter: An Example" for a sample of this process, page 139.)

4. Divide your class into pairs or trios and ask each to find an area of the room in which to work. Circulate among students, offering help as needed.

(Note: You will have already decided whether the Writer and Recipient are male or female. Don't allow students to fuss about playing a role of the opposite gender in their pairs or trios. Tell them that the important at this point is to imagine the story. If they choose, they can take turns playing the various roles.)

5. After approximately 5–8 minutes, assemble the class together again. Ask each pair or trio to show their stories to the rest of the class. After each group is finished, write their ideas on the blackboard.

    Students will imagine a diverse range of possibilities for this story—you can point out the similarities and differences between ideas presented and ask students for suggestions of how they can combine the various stories offered by various groups. However, you do not need to synthesize all these possibilities into a comprehensible whole at this time.

6. Later, after students have left for the day, copy the two lists from the blackboard on paper: 1) the clues you've collected from the Letter, and 2) the ideas for the story generated by the pairs or trios.

As best as you can, piece together students' story ideas to create an outline of a story. Attempt to include ideas contributed by each group. Make notes about where the class must make either/or decisions or other choices about the story, which they will do in Lesson 9. It's best to establish a limited number of choices for decision making, such as: "Was the ring stolen in Ireland or in Washington?" (See "The Mystery Letter: An Example.")

COMMENTARY:

In this lesson, students continue to assume responsibility for their drama. As teacher, your job is to facilitate the generation of students' ideas. At the same time, be clear about your own values and goals for your students. Point out to students the implications of their ideas, and, when necessary, set limits on story images that you believe do not serve to move the drama forward, help them deal with issues in their own lives, or connect students to an understanding of human experience.

For example, children are exposed to a tremendous amount of violence and pop culture images in the media and it's not unusual for them to include these elements in their story ideas. Often these images substitute clichés for deeper values. If pop culture images and use of guns and other forms of overt violence do not serve your educational goals, you can simply not allow these elements into your classroom drama. Of course, traditional folktales and fairy tales often include violence and as educators we should not shirk from addressing real issues in children's lives, including violence and death. But traditional tales are stories that teach lessons about life and the violence in them is usually in service to those lessons, unlike modern media images of violence that are often used only to titillate and excite.

Lesson 9
The Mystery Letter, Part 3

*The Designers Search
for the Recipient of the Letter* (30–45 minutes)

In this lesson, students create the story of the Stamp Designers in search of the intended Recipient of the Mystery Letter. Students work in small groups to improvise scenes while the rest of the class watches and makes suggestions. In this way, the entire class collaborates on playwriting. (Note: Substitute the names that your class has chosen for the Writer and Recipient.)

The Designers Search
for the Recipient of the Letter

CONTEXT:
"The Designers have discovered the story of what happened the last time the two people were together. They now use this information and other clues from the Mystery Letter in their attempt to find the intended recipient of the Letter."

SKILLS:
Story creation / playwriting
Artistic collaboration

MATERIALS / PREPARATION:
- The outline of the story as you've pieced it together from Lesson 8, including notes about what decisions, if any, your class must still make about the story

- Blackboard and chalk

PROCEDURE:

1. Review with students the outline of the story you have pieced together from the ideas they generated during Lesson 8. As you go over this outline with your class, continually ask students for agreement or clarification about the story and have them make necessary decisions—noted in your outline—either by discussion or by voting. (See "The Mystery Letter: An Example" for a sample of this procedure, page 139.)

2. When your class is in agreement about the story thus far, ask students to think of possibilities of how the Designers—acting as Postal Detectives—might proceed with seeking the Letter's intended Recipient in order to deliver the Letter to her or him. Write all students' suggestions on the blackboard.

   For example, your class had decided that "the book" was a clue that the Recipient is a librarian. A student suggests that the Designers go to the main library in their city and ask if any library staff members were born in Russia, the country from which the Mystery Letter was mailed. Or perhaps a student suggests calling telephone directory assistance in the city from which the Letter was sent to request the Writer's telephone number then calling the Writer to ask for the Recipient's address.

3. Choose one of the suggestions on the blackboard for an improvisation of "The Designers Search for the Letter Recipient." Select a few volunteers to improvise this idea in front of the class (the number of volunteers needed will depend on the scene chosen).

4. Ask all students for suggestions about how to begin this moment in the lives of the Designers. You will need to decide:

   • What students will play which roles

   • Where the action takes place

   • Where the various people enter/exit from

- What sets or props are needed and if so, what shall be used to show those objects (such as chairs, tables, and so forth).

    For example, the Designers go to the main branch of their city's library and ask if any staff members are from Russia. Three student volunteers are selected to play the roles: one Head Librarian, one Assistant Librarian, three Designers and one Library Patron. A table is placed center, as the library counter that the two Librarians stand behind, while the library patron sits in a chair to the side, reading a book. The Designers will enter from the right.

5. When everyone is in place and students are quiet, say, "Curtain up"—the signal to begin action and dialogue.

    Students who are in role improvise movement or dialogue for 10–15 seconds or until you see that they have either completed an idea or seem unsure of what to do next. When you think it's time to end the improvisation, say, "Curtain down."

6. Solicit comments about the improvisation. Ask students if they would like to change or add anything, such as changing something that was said or adding to the scene. Ask questions to lead students to consider details about the type of drama they want; for example, shall the Designers be sly or eager? Shall the Designers succeed in finding the Recipient or not? Do students want the other people in the story to oppose the Designers' efforts or to try to aid them?

7. At this point, you have several options depending on how your drama develops, how much time you have and how many students want to volunteer to improvise an idea. You can do any of the following:

- Continue to develop the current scene by repeating the scene with a new group of volunteers, making changes or additions as desired.

- Select a new idea from the blackboard (repeating Procedure Steps 4–6 with a new group of volunteers).
- Move on to step 8.

Make sure, however, that your class does not move forward too quickly. It's advisable to slow the pace of your drama by frequently pausing to ask questions and make statements that elicit thoughtfulness about your class's drama.

For example, pause the improvisation at any time by saying, "Freeze. When I tap each one of you on the shoulder, you will say aloud what your character is thinking." Or, simply stop the drama to ask questions such as: "What are the Designers' concerns at this moment?" Or, "Can you imagine what might happen if they fail in their mission to find the Recipient?" (Also see the Introduction to "The Mystery Letter," regarding slowing the pace of the drama.)

8. If desired, students can improvise a scene in which the Designers deliver the Letter to the Recipient. (You can also do this as part of Lesson 10.) Ask for suggestions, choose one idea and repeat steps 4–6.

Alternatively, your students' drama at this point might lead to a scene other than the Letter Delivery, such as another phase of action in the Designers' search for the Recipient. For example, students are satisfied that the Librarian's Assistant has slipped them the address of the Recipient and now want to go on to the next step of action in their drama. One student suggests that on the way to the Recipient's house, the Designers might get lost. The rest of the class is enthusiastic about improvising this new scene.

COMMENTARY:

The object of this activity is not to improvise complete scenes or even to become skillful at improvising. The goal is to collaborate in experimenting with ideas about what might happen in a particular moment of your drama. Feel free to stop the drama at any time in order to ask questions or to plan with your students what should happen next. If your students become excited and noisy, you can always call

"Freeze!" to stop the action. Then, with your thoughtful questions and statements, lead students to a more serious consideration of their drama.

You may hope that your students will decide that the Designer / Detectives are successful in locating the Recipient and delivering the Letter to her or him; however, it's fine if they decide otherwise. Be willing to go along with students' ideas for their drama even if they steer it in a different direction, such as deciding that the Recipient has died.

Lesson 10
The Mystery Letter, Part 4

Rendezvous at the Post Office (30–45 minutes)

On this day, the Writer of the Mystery Letter appears at the Post Office expecting to meet the Recipient. Students work as one, large group to improvise this moment in the lives of the Writer, the Recipient, the Stamp Designers, and any Post Office Workers and Customers who may be present. With this lesson, your class completes their collective playwriting of "The Mystery Letter." (Substitute the names for the Writer and Recipient that your class has chosen.)

Rendezvous at the Post Office

CONTEXT:
"Today is the day that the Writer of the Mystery Letter is scheduled to appear at the Post Office, hoping to rendezvous with the intended Recipient of the Letter. Let's see what happens."

SKILLS:
Commitment to believing in imaginary situations
Artistic collaboration

MATERIALS / PREPARATION:
- You may want to invite another adult (such as a parent of one of your students, a classroom aide or someone who is unknown to your students, such as your neighbor) to appear in role as the Writer of the Mystery Letter. It's also possible for either you or one of your students play the Writer. If you invite a guest to play this role, brief them beforehand (see Commentary).

- Your Post Office sign and classroom furniture arranged as the Post Office, in Lessons 2 and 3

- A ring (to be carried by the Writer) and a book (to be carried by the Recipient, if appropriate for your class' drama)

- A sound signal for "freeze," such as a bell or hand drum

- Students will begin by sitting, facing the Post Office area.

PROCEDURE:

If during your last drama session, your class was unable to complete the story of the Designers delivering—or failing to deliver—the Mystery Letter to the Recipient, do so at this time (see Lesson 9, Step 8).

1. Remind students that today is the day, according to the Mystery Letter, when the Writer is scheduled to appear at the Post Office in your city. Tell students that with this scene they will conclude the drama of the Mystery Letter. The Designers must complete their assignment as Postal Detectives so that they can return to their stamp design research and meet the deadline for entry in the postage stamp competition.

Today your class will work as an entire group to develop the story of this day at the Post Office. If any students are unable to focus their attention on this group activity, ask them to sit out and participate by watching and contributing ideas. Alternatively, you can ask half the students to watch and half to participate in role, then switch places.

By now, your class has already created a story about the last time the Writer and Recipient were together and about the Designer / Detectives' search for the Recipient. It will probably be clear at this point whether or not the Writer and Recipient will actually meet at the Post Office (that is, if the Designers were successful in finding her or him) and if so, what kind of reunion the two people will have. (Regardless of the decisions your class has made up until now, the Writer will appear at the post office on this appointed day in hopes of meeting the Recipient.)

2. Select students to be in role as the Writer (unless you have a guest present to be in this role), the Recipient (if indeed the Designers succeeded in finding her or him and delivering the Letter on time), and any other major characters your class has developed in their drama up to this point.

Ask the students who are playing these roles where each will be and what each will be doing when this moment begins: Will they be inside the Post Office or will they be just outside the door, about to enter? Will the Writer be waiting patiently by the counter or pacing around the room? Will the Recipient arrive on foot or in a car? Help each of these students find his beginning place and then ask them to sit down and watch while you help the rest of the students get situated.

3. Ask the remaining students to decide which group they want to be a part of: Post Office Workers, Customers, or Designer/ Detectives. Once the groups have been formed, help members of each group determine where they will be located in the scene when it begins and what they will be doing. When students are situated, ask them sit down and watch quietly while you help the others.

For example, you ask all students who wish to be Post Office Workers to raise their hands. Ask each one, "What type of work are you doing—serving customers, sorting mail, picking up mail-delivery bags? Where are you doing this work—behind the counter, over to one side of the Post Office area, entering through the front door?" The first student decides that she is helping customers from behind the counter. She goes to the counter and sits down while you continue with the next student.

4. When all students know what roles they are taking, where they will be located, and what action they will be doing, instruct students that the action will begin when you say, "Curtain up." Tell students that whenever they hear you make the "Freeze" signal—such as ringing a bell or beating a hand drum—they are to freeze in their positions. (This sound signal will give you, the

teacher, the ability to stop and start the drama as necessary, and it will help focus the group's attention when needed.)

5. When all students are quiet and ready to begin, say, "Curtain up." Feel free to stop and start the drama as often as needed to ask students:

for clarification of details—such as, *"Should the Writer be walking slowly or is he in a hurry?"*

for comments and critiques—such as, *"Did you like the way that Post Office Worker answered the Writer's question? Should we try it again a different way? How would you like her to answer this time?"*

for reflections about what is going on—such as, *"As a Designer/ Detective, what are you thinking about when you see these two people meet?"*

to repeat the action, including changes or additions, if desired

to focus students' attention

(See "The Mystery Letter: An Example" for a sample of this process.)

6. When students are satisfied with their conclusion of the drama you can, if you have the time and inclination, repeat the improvisation of this moment with different students playing various roles.

When you're finished, congratulate students on the completion of their drama of "The Mystery Letter" and tell them that the Designers will now be able to go back to their work of designing their postage stamp series.

COMMENTARY:

The educational goals of this drama curriculum include helping students develop their ability to focus attention on a group project and to collaborate effectively with others; however, don't be discouraged if some of your students are not capable of this as yet. If some of your students have difficulty staying focused on this large group improvisation, simply ask them to sit out and watch—they can learn a lot by watching and listening as well. You always have the option to call, "Freeze!" at any time to stop the drama and refocus your students' attention.

As noted in the Commentary for Lesson 9, your students may have decided that the Designer/Detectives are unsuccessful in finding the Recipient and delivering the Letter to her or him. Even if this is the case, you should still go ahead with the improvisation of the Writer's appearance at the Post Office in your city—perhaps the Writer waits all day at the Post Office and then leaves in disappointment; perhaps the Designers meet the Writer to give her or him some information they have discovered about the Recipient.

The Mystery Letter: An Example

Special thanks to the students of Eileen Aagaard's class at Syre Elementary in Shoreline, Washington, for their participation in developing this example.

The following is an example of how Lessons 7, 8, 9, and 10 might be presented to a first-grade class, along with students' possible responses. Be aware that this is only one possible outcome of the lesson and should not be considered a script that you or your students must follow.

PREPARATION OF THE MYSTERY LETTER'S ENVELOPE

The students in Ms. Greene's class have been working as Designers for the Sticky Sticker Design Company for several weeks, doing research at the Post Office for the postage stamp competition. One day, Ms. Greene tells her students that the Designers are soon to be approached by an Official from the Post Office, who will ask them to become temporary Postal Detectives in order to work on the case of a certain "Mystery Letter" that is undeliverable because the address is smudged.

Ms. Greene says, "If we get involved with this case, we'll have to do some detective work. We're stamp designers—are we capable of being detectives as well?" Her students are immediately enthusiastic about this project, but Ms. Greene wants them to consider the idea more closely. "What kind of things does a detective do?" For a few minutes, the class discusses what they know about the work of detectives.

DECIDING THE COUNTRY AND THE NAMES OF THE WRITER AND RECIPIENT

Now Ms. Greene says, "Since this is our own drama about the Mystery Letter, it's up to us to make a few decisions about it. First of all, what country would we like the Letter to come from?" Pointing to the classroom's world map, Ms. Greene says, "The Letter will either be mailed from Europe or from Africa. Let's take a vote." Two-thirds of the class vote for Europe. "Europe it is. Now, who can name some of the countries in Europe? I'll take the first eight suggestions." Eventually, the class decides that the country will be Ireland, as one of the students has relatives there. (Meanwhile, Ms. Greene makes a mental note to pursue a geography lesson in conjunction with the drama curriculum.)

Ms. Greene says, "We'll say that the Writer of the letter is a male and the person the letter is addressed to is a female. Does anybody know an Irish name for a boy?" "Juan!" calls out one student. "No," says Ms. Greene, "'Juan' is a Spanish or Latin American name." "Patrick!" cries another student. "Yes, Patrick is a good Irish name," Ms. Greene replies. "Now, how about an Irish girl's name?" Before long, the names 'Patrick and Irene O'Neil' are decided upon for the letter Writer and Recipient.

PREPARING THE MYSTERY LETTER

Later, after her students have gone home for the day, Ms. Greene prepares an envelope addressed to Irene O'Neil in Shoreline, Washington (where Ms. Greene's school is), from Patrick O'Neil in Dublin, Ireland. Dipping her finger in some water, Ms. Greene smudges the ink on Irene's street address to make it illegible.

Next, she handwrites a copy of the Mystery Letter, adding a date for the rendezvous at the Post Office (the date her class will do "The Mystery Letter: Part 4.") Ms. Greene copies the letter onto a plastic transparency and reserves an overhead projector from the school's media center. Lastly, she photocopies the information the Post Office Official will need for "The Mystery Letter: Part 1" from her drama curriculum book and goes to visit Rae, the school's librarian who will be taking the role of the Official. "You don't have to be an actor," Ms. Greene tells Rae. "Just be officious in your manner and don't make up any details about the Letter that will influence the students' choices for the story."

The Mystery Letter, Part 1
The Designers Become Postal Detectives

The next day when Ms. Greene's students come into class after lunch, the "Sticky Sticker Company" sign is on the wall, along with their company's design award certificates. On each student's desk is a pencil and blank piece of paper. "Good afternoon, Designers!" Ms. Greene greets the students. "As your secretary, it's my job to remind you that we have a deadline coming up for the postage stamp competition." To help them get started on their stamp designs, Ms. Greene asks students to name aloud all the Post Office activities they've experienced during previous drama lessons. Some of the activities students mention include: doing warm-ups at the Training School, greeting people at the Post Office while speaking in gibberish, and delivering mail during the Movement Story.

Ms. Greene then directs her students to sit at their desks and begin drawing stamp design ideas (in role as the Designers) while she circulates among them (as their Secretary). She encourages them to remember their Post Office "research" and to make connections between those activities and their task of designing stamps. "What are some of the things we did at the Post Office?" she asks Evan, who is poking Stefano with his pencil. "Uh…we made a stamping machine," he says. Ms. Greene asks, "Does that sound like something you would like to draw for your stamp design?" Evan perks up. "I'm real good at drawing trucks!" he says. "A mail truck would be a good subject for a stamp design," suggests Ms. Greene and Evan begins to draw one.

THE POST OFFICE OFFICIAL ARRIVES
After about fifteen minutes Ms. Greene gives a quick call to the school library, and a minute later there's a knock on the door. Rae comes briskly into the room saying, "Hello, I'm the Post Office Supervisor and I need to talk to the Stamp Designers about something very important!" She explains her mission and the students,

who have been anticipating her request, quickly agree to become Postal Detectives. After the official "swearing in" ceremony, Rae gives the Mystery Letter to one of the students, thanks the Designers for their help, and leaves.

"I'll make a copy of the Letter so we can read it together," says Ms. Greene as she pulls the plastic transparency out of her desk and sets up the overhead projector. Together, students read the Letter aloud. "Why are some of the letters bigger than others?" asks Katie. "I don't know," shrugs Ms. Greene. "What do you think?" The students all talk at once, eager with ideas, and it's not long before the class deciphers the message hidden in the secret code: "Ma's will." Ms. Greene looks at the clock and realizes it's time for them to stop and go to PE. "Keep thinking of possibilities of what the Letter is all about and we'll continue tomorrow."

The Mystery Letter, Part 2
What Happened the Last Time the Writer and Recipient Were Together

The next day, the class brainstorms a list of the clues they can glean from the Letter while Ms. Greene writes them on the board. She tells her students that they will now make up stories, using these clues, about what happened the last time Patrick and Irene were together. She writes on the blackboard "Who, What, Where" and explains that these words will help students make some decisions about their stories. "Who are these two people and how are they related to each other? Are they sister and brother, wife and husband, father and daughter?" Ms. Greene goes on to elaborate: "What happens in this story? Is it something that Patrick and Irene see, something that they hear, or perhaps something that happens to them? Where are they when it happens? Are they at home or some other place?"

Ms. Greene tells her students "You will work with one or two other classmates and together imagine a story about the last time

Patrick and Irene were together. Decide who will play the role of Patrick and who will play Irene and then act out your story. You can switch roles at any time and you can also stop your story at any time to invent new ideas."

STORY CREATION IN PAIRS AND TRIOS

Ms. Greene asks her students to divide themselves into pairs or trios and to find a place in the classroom to work on their stories. It takes a few minutes for everyone to find a group, and for each group to get situated. As Ms. Greene circulates among her students she sees that some of them are immediately engaged in creating a story, such as the pair of girls who begin concocting an elaborate story about losing a diamond ring in a movie theater. However, other students are having trouble understanding the assignment or staying on task. Artie and Jason are wrestling on the floor.

"Well, guys, what do you think might have happened the last time Patrick and Irene were together?" The two boys look blank. Ms. Greene tries again: "Okay, let's think about the ring mentioned in the Letter. Is there anything special about this ring?" Artie gets inspired, "It's worth a billion dollars!" "So it's a very expensive ring," Ms. Greene goes on. "Was there something about the ring that Patrick and Irene saw or something that they heard?" "They saw a robber!" says Jason. "I want to be the robber!" cries Artie. "No, me—it was my idea!" Jason retorts. Ms. Greene reminds them that they can always take turns. The boys readily agree and begin to create an action-filled story about Patrick being robbed of his ring.

SHARING STORY IDEAS WITH THE GROUP

After a few minutes, Ms. Greene calls the class together again and asks students to sit in one large circle. One at a time, each pair or trio acts out their story in front of the class. There are a variety of stories, including: Patrick and his mother being robbed at home and the mother being killed; the two people in their mansion after their mother's funeral, discussing her will; the two people being robbed in a store by a robber disguised as a policeman; and one story about

Patrick and Irene's mother losing her ring in a movie theater. A couple of groups have nothing to show because they weren't sure of what to do, but Ms. Greene isn't concerned because she can see that these students are learning by seeing the work of the other groups.

Afterwards, as the class is departing to go to Music class, Rachel says to Ms. Greene, "You know, Patrick's address is on the envelope. We could just write to him and ask him for Irene's address." "Hmm...," says Ms. Greene.

The Mystery Letter, Part 3
The Designers Search
for the Recipient of the Letter

Over the weekend, Ms. Greene pieces together all the stories that students had generated thus far. She is pleased that some part of each group's ideas can be made to fit into the story's overall outline. She writes in her notes that the class still needs to determine: 1) whether the mother was killed by a robber or of other causes, 2) whether the robbery took place in Ireland or Tacoma, and 3) how Patrick got the ring back after it had been stolen by the robber.

CLARIFYING THE STORY OUTLINE
In class, Ms. Greene reads her outline for the story, "Patrick and Irene are brother and sister who live with their mother in a mansion in Ireland. Is that right?" Students agree. She continues, "Their mother has a diamond ring that is later stolen—either from their mansion in Ireland or from a store in Tacoma, Washington. Which shall it be—Ireland or Tacoma? Remember, Patrick has the ring now and we know he sent the Letter from Ireland." The class decides that it makes more sense that the robbery take place in Ireland. One student, though, suggests that the ring could have been stolen in Tacoma, after which the robber went to Ireland.

"In that case, how does Patrick get the ring back from the robber?" asks Ms. Greene.

No one has an immediate answer. Jeff says, "I know! The ring was stolen from their mansion in Ireland. But the robber had a hole in his pocket, and it fell to the ground and Patrick found it." The rest of the class is enthusiastic about this idea and Ms. Greene continues going over the outline with her class until the entire story is pieced together. Katie, however, is disturbed about something. "Does the mother have to be killed by the robber?" she asks. Ms. Greene says, "That's what the class voted for, but I can see you feel uncomfortable about it." Ms. Greene turns to the rest of the class. "Should we change it?" "No!" cry a couple of students but Justin looks thoughtful. "She could be so scared of the robber that she has a heart attack." Katie is relieved—it was the violence of an attack on the mother that bothered her, not the death itself. The rest of the class readily agrees with this slight change in the story. "Fantastic!" exclaims Ms. Greene, "This is true collaboration!"

THE DESIGNER/DETECTIVES SEARCH
FOR THE RECIPIENT

Now Ms. Greene asks the class to consider all the possible ways in which the Designer/Detectives could proceed with finding Irene in order to deliver the Letter to her. "Yesterday, Rachel thought of writing to Patrick for Irene's address. What do you think of that?" At first the class is enthusiastic, but Ms. Greene wants them to consider this proposal more carefully. "In the Letter Patrick says he will be at the Shoreline Post Office on October 15th." Nick looks at the classroom calendar. "That's tomorrow!" he cries. Nick thinks for a moment and says, "There won't be time to mail him a letter and get one back before tomorrow." "Good thinking, Nick," says Ms. Greene. "What else could we do?" Stefano thinks of calling Patrick. "There's no phone number on the envelope," Ms. Greene points out. Andrea thinks of calling directory assistance for Patrick's number and the rest of the class agrees with her idea.

"We will need someone to play Patrick," says Ms. Greene. "Me! Me!" several of the students cry, eagerly raising their hands. Ms. Greene randomly selects a few students to come to the front of the room to play the roles of Patrick, the Telephone Operator, and three Designers. These last three students begin to argue about who will make the actual phone call, but Ms. Greene says, "Have you ever heard of a conference call?"

"Let's have the Designers call from their studio, over here," suggests Ms. Greene. "Where will we have Patrick stand?" "He won't be there because he's in Ireland," says Tiffanie. Ms. Greene explains, "We can have a 'split screen,' like they have on TV, showing two places at the same time." Andrew decides that, as Patrick, he will be just about to leave his mansion to go to the airport, carrying his suitcase. The three Designers decide to sit together around a table, each with her or his own imaginary telephone. Meanwhile, the student who is to play the Operator wanders around in confusion. Ms. Greene suggests that he stand in the middle, between the two scenes. The rest of the class sits on the floor to watch this scene.

CURTAIN UP
When everyone is quiet, Ms. Greene says, "Curtain up." At first, the students in the scene look at each other, unsure of what to do. Finally, Andrea, one of the Designers, says, "I have an idea! Let's call Patrick for Irene's address. Ring!! Ring!!" Andrew (Patrick) picks up his phone, "Hello?"

"Freeze!" cries Ms. Greene. "Remember, Patrick's telephone number isn't on the envelope. Think about what the Designers can do to find out his number. Ready? Continue." The students proceed to improvise a scene of calling the Operator and then reaching Patrick, who tells them Irene's address. "Curtain down." says Ms. Greene. "Well, class, what do you think? Is there anything you want to change about this scene?"

"It's fine," says one student. "Let's give the letter to Irene!" cries another. Ms. Greene wants to make sure the pace of the drama doesn't go too fast, but she can sense that her students are ready to move on to the next part of their drama. "Shall we go now to the scene in which the Designers deliver the Letter to Irene?" "Yeah!" cry several students.

DELIVERING THE LETTER

Ms. Greene quickly determines that with the time left in their drama period, they can probably do this next scene three times, with seven to eight students playing the roles each time. This will give all students a chance to participate. She calls on six volunteers to play the Designers and one to play Irene. Several students busily set up several chairs to be the couch in Irene's living room. Ms. Greene asks the Designers, "Will you arrive on foot or in a car?" "VRROOM!!!" yells Kyle as he races around the room. Ms. Greene sees that in order to help Kyle control his boundless energy, there needs to be a limit set on physical movement. She makes a quick decision: "Okay, let's say the scene begins as the Designers are walking up to Irene's front door." She gives these students the Mystery Letter in its envelope.

When Ms. Greene says, "Curtain up," students improvise the moment of the Designers arriving at Irene's house, ringing her doorbell, and handing her the Letter, while the rest of the class watches. Next, Ms. Greene calls on a second group to try the same scene and asks them, "Is there anything you would like to do differently this time?" Several students want the scene to last longer and Alex says, "Irene invites them in to tea." This group improvises the scene and after that, a third group does so as well, this time continuing the scene through the moment when Irene leaves the house to go to the Post Office to meet Patrick.

The Mystery Letter, Part 4
Rendezvous at the Post Office

"Today is the day that Patrick will arrive at the Post Office in Shoreline," Ms. Greene greets her students the next morning. She has written "U.S. POST OFFICE" on the blackboard and arranged a couple of tables at the front of the room to indicate the Post Office counter (as she did for Lessons 2 and 3). "Today, our entire class will improvise the moment of the meeting between Patrick and Irene. If anyone has trouble concentrating on the scene, I will ask them to sit and watch instead. First, we need a Patrick and an Irene."

Many eager hands go up and Ms. Greene randomly selects two students. She gives Patrick a rhinestone ring, and to Irene she gives a small book (Ms. Greene's class had previously determined that both people are to be married soon. Irene urgently needs the ring for her wedding and Patrick needs the family prayer book for his). "When this moment begins will Patrick be at the Post Office already or has he not arrived yet? And where exactly is Irene?" Ms. Greene helps the students playing Patrick and Irene to get situated just outside the imaginary doorway of the Post Office.

Next, Ms. Greene asks the remaining students to decide which group they want to be a part of: Post Office Workers, Customers, or Designers. Once the groups have been formed, members of each group determine where they will be located in the scene when it begins and what they will be doing. Although she tries to do this in a calm, methodical fashion, for several moments the classroom is filled with noisy excitement as students mill around, all talking at once. Ms. Greene turns the classroom light switch off for a few seconds to get her students' attention. "Without talking," she says to them. "Go to where you are in the Post Office when the scene begins."

CURTAIN UP

Eventually, all students get situated in the Post Office and are involved in their characters' actions. Ms. Greene calls the class to attention again and says, "Curtain up." Within a few seconds, several students are talking at once and a couple of them are excitedly pushing chairs around the room. "Freeze!" calls Ms. Greene. "When we do a group improvisation, everyone needs to concentrate. Where should everyone's focus be in this scene?" Some students looks confused. Alex says, "On Patrick and Irene?" "Yes," says Ms. Greene. "The central focus of this moment is Patrick arriving at the Post Office to meet Irene. This time, everyone be aware of the meeting between Patrick and Irene. Ready? Curtain up."

Patrick soon arrives at the Post Office and mills around for a few moments until Cyndy enters with several Designers in tow. "Come, chauffeur!" she cries as she sweeps into the room. "I'm her chauffeur!" says Sara, happily. "She has a limousine!" Irene comes up to Patrick, and they both mumble something and then exchange the ring and the book. "I have to go now!" Irene cries. "Where's my limousine? Chauffeur!" She and Sara exit and Ms. Greene calls, "Curtain down."

Ms. Greene now asks everyone to sit down and then she asks for comments about the scene. "Irene is rich," comments one student. "Because she owns a diamond ring shop," says another. "I couldn't hear what they said," says Nick. "They have to talk louder." The students seem to like the scene. "Would you like to try it again with a different Patrick and Irene?" Her students are eager, so Ms. Greene selects two more students to play Patrick and Irene. "Remember what Nick said about not being able to hear what Patrick and Irene said to each other. This time, Patrick and Irene should speak loudly and clearly so we can all hear them."

The class repeats the scene. "This time," asks Ms. Greene. "Should the Writer be walking slowly or is he in a hurry?" Jacob decides he will be in a hurry to get the book from Irene. Ms. Greene muses, "I wonder what it would be like to not see my brother or sister for a long time and then to see them again...." Rachel looks thoughtful. "I would be glad," she says. During the next improvisation of the scene, Ms. Greene again calls "Freeze!" She turns to the students playing the Designer/Detectives and asks them, "What are you thinking about when you see these two people meet?"

When it's time to end their drama period for the day, Ms. Greene says, "Now the Designers are able to go back to work on their designs for the postage stamp competition."

PART IV

INTERPRETING, RECORDING, AND PRESENTING THE DESIGNERS' EXPERIENCES

In Part IV students use several dramatic forms to explore, interpret, and record their experiences as Designers and to share those experiences with others. They analyze and reflect on their experiences and communicate their thoughts and feelings through public speaking ("TV Interview"), and further explore the designing of postage stamps through tableaux and drawing ("Living Postage Stamps" and "Postage Stamp Designs").

In these lessons students have the opportunity to observe the effect of their words and actions on others by presenting their ideas to their classmates. The section "Public Sharing Event" gives suggestions on how to present some of the drama forms the students have created in Part III to an outside audience—perhaps to another class or to their parents. Students will enjoy the chance to "show off" while you, the teacher, will appreciate the experience as one in which students monitor the effectiveness of their communication skills and of the symbols they've created (in language, movement, and story) to explicate their ideas. The public presentation suggested here is intended to be informal and enjoyable, with the focus being on a positive experience for your students in "making their private thoughts public."

Lesson 11
Reflection and Sharing

Reflection and Sharing: *TV Interview*   (15–20 minutes)

Reflection and Sharing: *TV Interview*

CONTEXT:

"A local TV station wants to interview our design company about our stamp design research and our role in solving the case of 'The Mystery Letter.'"

SKILLS:

Awareness and expression of inner thoughts, feelings and values
Public presentation: the outward expression of inner thoughts, feelings and values

MATERIALS / PREPARATION:

- Before the class arrives, set up an area where individuals will stand to be interviewed, including the following:
  - carpet square, platform, sturdy box, or any other way to designate a small area for interviews
  - microphone, either real or pretend (such as a toy or a decorated cardboard tube)
  - tape recorder and blank cassette tape or video camera to record the interview (Note: You may wish to have an audio or video recording of the interview to include in your Public Sharing Event.)

- Prepare a list of interview questions based on the kinds of learning you want your class to experience. (See list of suggested types of questions at the end of the Procedure. For more about teaching goals and asking questions, see Commentary at the end of this lesson and the section, "Asking Questions," in Chapter 2.)

- (Optional) You can arrange in advance to have another adult in role as the recording engineer or The Interviewer. If so, brief your guest beforehand about his role. If another adult is to play The Interviewer, she or he will need your list of questions in advance.

- Initially, you will receive a telephone message that will "set the stage" for this lesson. You have the option of arranging in advance with another adult to call you on your classroom telephone or to send you a telephone message from the office. (You can also choose to simply announce to your class that you have received a telephone message.)

PROCEDURE:

1. You receive a telephone message (the telephone rings or you receive a note from the office). Announce to your class:

   "A local TV station has called us, (name of your design company). They have heard about our stamp design research and about how we helped to solve the case of 'The Mystery Letter.' They're coming right now to interview us on TV!"

2. Show students the interviewing area and microphone, then brief them on TV etiquette: During the interview no extraneous sounds or movements should be made as they will be heard and seen on the air. You or another adult will play the Interviewer. Students will answer your questions in their role as members of the stamp design company. Encourage all students to participate but if some students are reluctant to speak, allow them to simply watch.

   One way to set up the interview is to have students line up at the stage when they want to answer a question. Students will then step up to the stage one at a time to answer questions.

   You may alternatively choose to have the students remain seated at their desks. After each question is asked you, or another adult playing the Interviewer, can bring the microphone to each student in turn. Another possible format is to have all students sit in a circle. After each question is asked, pass the microphone around the circle so that everyone gets a turn to answer. In either format, students may say, "Pass" if they don't wish to answer a question.

3. Turn on the tape recorder or video camera and begin the interview by saying (or having the adult in role as the Interviewer say), "To all our listeners: This is television station KXYZ and here with us today are a remarkable group of stamp designers." Proceed with the interview: Ask a question and allow several (or all) students to answer before continuing with the next question. This allows students to compare and contrast their answers with the answers of others. (See list of suggested types of questions at the end of this Procedure.)

4. When the interview session is over, or at a later time, replay the taped interview for the students so they can see or hear themselves "on the air."

INTERVIEW QUESTIONS:

The following is a suggested list of types of questions appropriate for "TV Interview." (Sample questions are from "The Mystery Letter: An Example" and from our own experiences in presenting these lessons and should be taken as examples only. Your own questions may be quite different.) The words in **bold italic** are particularly useful phrases for eliciting reflective answers. Be sure to include questions in your interview that require students to reflect on their research as stamp designers as well as on their role in solving the case of "The Mystery Letter."

To encourage students to interpret their experiences and to select significant points:

"**What has been the most interesting part** of your research on postal workers?"

"**What is the most important part** of your work as a stamp designer and postal detective?"

"What part of the story of 'The Mystery Letter' stands out for you? Why?"

To encourage students to consider alternatives and make suppositions:

> "*What do you imagine* might have happened if you had been unable to deliver the Mystery Letter?"

> "*What might your stamp designs have looked like if you had not had this experience as a postal detective?*"

To ask for a personal response about either the experience itself or about students' relationships to others:

> "*What were your concerns* when you first read the letter?"

> "*What were you thinking* when you saw the two family members meet at last at the Post Office (or when one family member failed to show up at the Post Office)."

> "*What was the easiest or most difficult part* of piecing together the story of 'The Mystery Letter'?"

To encourage students to make value judgments:

> "*Do you think it was right* to open and read someone else's letter?"

> "*Do you imagine that stamp designs will be different now because of your work?*"

> "*Should you win the competition, your stamps will be seen all over the world. What do you think the unique story you have told with your stamps will tell the world about the United States?*"

To clarify the students' responses for the teacher:

> "*Do I understand you to mean* that you disagreed with the group's decision to read the letter?"

> "*Are you saying* that you would solve this case differently next time?"

COMMENTARY:

This lesson creates a formal yet nonthreatening way for students to speak their private thoughts, feelings, and experiences in public. Public speaking requires clarity of language, good "stage presence," and a clear voice that is loud enough to be heard by all. Giving students the option of not speaking creates a safe atmosphere for them to contribute freely, without pressure. By using a structured format of either having students line up to answer questions, bringing the microphone to each student in turn, or passing the microphone around a circle, you assure that all students will receive an opportunity to speak.

Carefully prepare your interview questions beforehand. Reread the section on "Asking Questions" in Chapter 2 and be clear about your educational goals for this lesson as you formulate your list of questions. "TV Interview" has been placed at this point in the curriculum to give students the opportunity to interpret and evaluate their experiences as Stamp Designers researching Postal Workers and their role in solving the case of "The Mystery Letter." This activity also gives the teacher an opportunity to monitor any changes in the students' learning process as a result of these experiences.

In order for students to feel they can speak freely, do not evaluate their responses. Take care to not imply value judgments or an expectation of a "right" answer in your role as Interviewer. Be aware of nonverbal signals you may be giving through your body language and vocal intonation. Maintain a safe atmosphere for answering questions by using the bland, subjective, nonemotional wording and vocal intonation of a TV interviewer. Don't rush students to answer questions immediately—give them plenty of time to think. Don't be afraid to allow for pauses of 10 or more seconds while students are formulating their answers.

VARIATIONS:

Individual students can take a turn playing the Interviewer. Although their questions may not be as focused as those on your carefully planned list, the experience of asking questions will help them develop communication skills.

Formal interviews can be used to elicit other kinds of information from your students, helping you discover what they know or understand. For example, after a field trip to see a play, students can be interviewed about what they remember and understand about the play. Or, after a discussion about classroom rules, students can be interviewed about what they think about both the rules and the discussion process.

Lesson 12
Creating Stamps

Tableaux: *Living Postage Stamps #1*   (30–45 minutes)

Tableaux: *Living Postage Stamps #1*

Context:

"Now it's time to design our stamps for submission to the Postmaster General. Let's make stamp designs that tell the story of how we helped the Post Office solve the case of the Mystery Letter."

SKILLS:
Expressive use of body and movement
Collaboration and negotiation with others

MATERIALS / PREPARATION:
- Before this lesson begins you will need to make a list of ten to twelve events that can be depicted as a series of narrated tableaux (the "stamp designs") from the story your class created about "The Mystery Letter." The events might include the "swearing in" of the Designers as Postal Detectives, scenes describing what happened between the two family members, and the final scene at the Post Office. Be sure to include several large group scenes as well as scenes between two or three characters. Make sure your list includes enough scenes for each student in the class to have an opportunity to play a major character, as well as to participate in one or two group scenes.

- Write a narrative script by describing each scene on the list above in a single, simple sentence that will also serve as a narration, to be spoken either by yourself or by a student volunteer. For example: "The Designers are being sworn in as Postal Detectives by the Post Office Official." If the narration will be read by students, make sure it is written in language appropriate to your class's reading level.

- Number each line of narration in order, leaving a few spaces between each sentence for notes. (You will want to jot down, for example, the names of students who will participate in each scene.) If students will be reading the narration, make an extra copy of your narrative script for the narrators to use in class and another copy for the next step, below. (For a sample narrative script, see "The Mystery Letter: An Example.")

- If students are to speak the narration from memory, make an extra copy of the script. Cut out each student's narration line(s) and paste it to a note to be sent home with the student asking his parents to help their child memorize his line(s).

- Copy the narrative script on the blackboard or large piece of butcher paper. Leave space between each sentence for writing the names of the students participating in the scene.

- Write all students' names, each on a separate slip of paper, and then place the slips in two bowls or other containers—one for the boys' names and one for the girls' names

- A sound signal, such as a rain stick or bell

- A small "stage" area, large enough for students to perform limited movement, and an area for audience members to sit and view the students who are performing.

PROCEDURE:

1. Tell the class that their design company will be creating a series of twelve (or whatever number of events you have listed) stamp designs to submit to the Postmaster General. Explain that they will show their stamp designs with live "models," in a series of tableaux (as they did for "Family Photo Album" in Lesson 5).

- Look at the first event on your list and determine how many characters will be needed to show the scene. Select students to be the characters in the scene (stamp design) by choosing names at random out of the bowls. For example, if the scene has two characters, a man and a woman, draw one name from the boys' container and one from the girls' container to determine who will play the scene.

- If students will be speaking the narration sentences, also draw a name at random to be the scene's narrator.
- Ask the students whose names were drawn, as well as the narrator, to come to the performing space. (Alternatively, you may choose to narrate the scenes yourself.)
- Write on the blackboard, in the space underneath the scene description, the names of the students who have been selected for the scene. You should later transfer these names onto your own narrative script.

2. Tell the performers that they will be creating stamp designs depicting the first event on the list by making a frozen tableau as they did for the family photos (Lesson 5). Give the performers a minute to organize their stamp design tableau, allowing the rest of the class to contribute ideas about where each character should be and what he or she should be doing. Students may use simple sets or props as needed, such as a chair, a table, or a piece of paper.

3. When the group has organized their tableau, explain the following procedure:

- You will say "Freeze," at which time the group will freeze in their tableau.
- You, or a student narrator, will read the narration sentence while the scene remains frozen.
- After pausing for another 3–5 seconds, you will give the sound signal. At this sound, students "Unfreeze" and then go to the audience area to sit down.
- Repeat steps 1–3 for the next scene on your list.

4. Do the procedure described above. If you have approximately twelve scenes/stamp designs planned, you may not have time to develop all of them in this 30–45 minute period (some students may become restless as well). This is fine—you will be able to finish planning your scenes/stamp designs in Lesson 13.

COMMENTARY:

This lesson provides students with a chance to mentally review their experiences as Designers solving the case of "The Mystery Letter." You can always help groups with their tableaux by coaching with questions and suggestions such as: "What expression was on your face when you were sworn in by the Postmaster General?" or "Perhaps the family would pass the serving bowl around the table."

Students will appreciate the fairness of casting scenes through random selection. Having separate bowls for boys' and girls' names makes it simple to cast male and female roles, but it is also possible to put all names in one bowl if your students are open to being cast as characters of the opposite gender. You can remind them that, in the early days of theater, women's roles were always played by men. It's not unusual, either, for women to play men's roles.

Some students may become restless when they are not actively participating in a scene. For this reason, it is important to make sure that every student has a featured role in at least one scene and is also part of one or two group scenes. Encourage students to become involved even when they are not performing by asking for their help in designing each tableau. Ask questions such as: "Do these positions look right to you?" "Can you see Jeff's face from where he's stand-ing?" "Where do you think the chair should be?" and so on. You will find that all students will become more attentive and enthusiastic once the full stamp design sequence begins to take shape, and they can see the events of their story unfolding.

VARIATIONS:

At another time, show students reproductions of actual postage stamps and have them recreate those designs as "Living Postage Stamps." You can also do this activity using famous paintings or illustrations from children's books. Try having students do "Living Book Reports" where groups create tableaux of scenes from a story, then briefly make the scenes come to life.

Lesson 13
Creating Stamps, continued

A. Tableaux & Pantomime: *Living Postage Stamps #2* (30–45 min.)
B. Drawing: *Postage Stamp Designs*   (as time permits)

A. Tableaux and Pantomime:
Living Postage Stamps #2

CONTEXT:
"Today we'll finish planning our stamp designs, then practice showing them in order, as we will for the Postmaster General. Then we'll have a chance to make drawings of our stamp designs as well."

SKILLS:
Ability to sequence events
Organization and synthesis of ideas

MATERIALS / PREPARATION:
- See Lesson 12: "Creating Stamps"

- The room arranged so that students can sit at their desks or tables to draw stamp designs after the tableaux activity

PROCEDURE:
1. Remind students of the stamp design tableaux they created in Lesson 12. If you did not complete setting the tableaux for all the stamp designs on your list in Lesson 12, begin where you left off and follow steps 1–4 of the Procedure for that lesson, guiding students in creating the tableaux for the remaining stamp designs on your list.

2. Tell students that they will now practice showing all of the stamp designs in order, just as they will when they present their

designs to the Postmaster General. Explain that this time, after the narrator has introduced the stamp, the scene will come to life for a few seconds. Ask students to look at the list on the board as you review the order of the stamp designs.

3. Explain the following procedure:
   - You will call out "Stamp #1." The performers and narrator (if you will not be reading the narration) for that design will quickly come to the performing area and take their frozen positions in the tableau they have planned.
   - The narrator (or you) will speak the sentence describing the stamp design.
   - After the narrator has spoken, the tableau will "come to life," as performers pantomime the actions of the characters in the scene, speaking if they wish. Optionally, students can decide to have their tableau remain frozen if that seems the most appropriate way to present a particular scene.
   - You will allow the scene to either move or remain frozen for 3-10 seconds, then give a sound signal (rain stick or bell). At this signal students move to positions for the next scene. Students who will not be in the following scene either sit in the audience area or "backstage," areas that you establish at the sides of the stage where students can sit in small groups when they're not performing. Maintaining focus and remaining quiet while backstage is an important drama skill.
   - You will call "Stamp #2," and the procedure will be repeated with the next group.

4. Do the procedure described above, emphasizing smooth transitions between designs so that the sequence of the story is clear.

5. If time permits, go immediately to Activity B. Alternatively, give students an opportunity to draw (or finish drawing) their stamp designs at a later time.

B. Drawing: *Postage Stamp Designs*

MATERIALS / PREPARATION:

- 8" x 11" sheets of paper, cut in half widthwise; at least one half-sheet per student

- Crayons, markers or colored pencils for all students

PROCEDURE:

Have students go to their desks or tables. Explain that each student will draw at least one stamp design from your list: one on each half-sheet of paper, each design reflecting one of the scenes on the list. Assign each student one scene to draw, preferably one in which they are performing. Make sure that each scene on your list will be drawn by at least one student, as these drawings will be displayed as part of the Public Sharing Event. (Several scenes may have more than one drawing, depending on the number of students in your class.) Ask students to write the Stamp # on their drawings. Allow students as much time as needed to complete their drawings, giving them additional time later or on another day if necessary.

COMMENTARY:

This lesson provides students with the opportunity to refine the tableaux they began creating in Lesson 12, and to add the element of pantomime to their scenes. Repeating and revising their work gives students a taste of being involved in the process of a rehearsal. Being able to run through the entire sequence of stamp designs smoothly will give students a sense of pride in their work, and it will solidify the events of their "Mystery Letter" story in their minds.

Public Sharing Event

Receiving the Contract   (30–45 minutes)

At this point in the drama curriculum your students are ready to show some of their drama activities to others. Plan an event in which your students can share some or all of the drama forms they've created in Part IV with a small group of people, such as another class. This public sharing should be an informal and enjoyable gathering, with the emphasis on creating a positive experience for the participating students (as opposed to a stressful "performance").

Receiving the Contract

CONTEXT:
"Post Office officials are coming to judge our stamp designs for the contest and to learn about our involvement in the case of 'The Mystery Letter.'"

SKILLS:
Public presentation: the outward expression of inner thoughts and feelings

MATERIALS / PREPARATION:
- (Optional) Invite an adult to be in role as the Postmaster General during the sharing event. Be sure to brief this volunteer on presenting the contract at the end of the event (see Step 6 of the Procedure, below). Alternatively, you can ask someone from the your school to deliver the contract to your classroom at the end of the Public Sharing Event.

- See below for each activity

- A "contract," to be awarded to the Designers at the end of the public presentation. You may photocopy the example below, adding the current date and the name of your class's stamp design company, or you may create a contract of your own.

(current date)

In acknowledgment of their superior stamp design submission, the Postmaster General of the United States of America hereby awards to:

(name of your stamp design company)

a contract to design a series of postage stamps, to be produced by the United States Postal Service, with the theme:

"Honoring U.S. Postal Workers"

Stamps will receive national circulation for one year.

Respectfully Yours,

_____

Postmaster General of the United States of America

PROCEDURE:

1. Make arrangements for another class to visit your classroom. (See Variations, below, regarding inviting students' parents to your sharing event.) Inform the teacher of the visiting class about the Designers' research on U.S. Postal Workers and about their experience with "The Mystery Letter." The visiting class will be present as Post Office officials who have come to see the stamp designs and to hear about the role of the designers as postal detectives. (The visiting students do not need to know more than this, nor are they required to "act a role.")

2. Tell your class that U.S. Post Office officials are coming to see the class's stamp designs and learn about their work as postal detectives. The Designers will present their "Living Postage Stamps." Decide with your class which of the other following activities or items they wish to share (choose any or all) and make the necessary preparations.

LIVE ACTION:

Title: *Living Postage Stamps* (Lessons 12 and 13)
Materials / Preparation:
- Post order of stamp designs with names of performers for each design (from Lessons 12 and 13) on either the blackboard or a large piece of butcher paper
- Space arranged for both performers and audience members
- Rehearsal, as needed (30–45 minutes are suggested)
  (Note: During rehearsals and during the Public Sharing Event the students can follow the posted list of stamp designs and will be responsible for being on stage at the appropriate time. The teacher, therefore, does not need to call out the number of each stamp design. Remind student narrators (if you have any) to memorize their lines. You will need to encourage narrators and speaking performers to speak loudly, slowly, and clearly so their words can be heard and understood by the audience. (See Part VII: Play Production, section on "Basic Acting Skills" for ideas on how to encourage students to project their voices.)

Title: *Movement Machine* (Lesson 2)
Materials / Preparation:
- Space arranged for both performers and audience members
- Review activity (if needed)

Title: *Soundscape* (Lesson 4)
Materials / Preparation:
- Have students practice conducting sounds (see "Sound Signals" procedure, Lesson 4)

- Divide story into as many sound cues as there are performing students
- Have students stand in a line, facing the audience
- Rehearse story as needed with each student in line taking a turn to conduct one sound cue as you narrate

  (Note: This is a good audience participation activity, with everyone in the audience joining in to make the sounds as the students conduct.)

RECORDING:
Title: *TV Interview* (Lesson 11)
Materials / Preparation:
- Audio or video cassette recording of interviews
- Audio or video cassette player
- (Optional) Written list of interview questions

DISPLAY: (Placed on tables or tacked on bulletin boards)
- Your Stamp Design Company sign
- The Design Company's certificates of award (See "Starting Out")
- Original e-message from Postmaster/copy of the Designers' reply
- "Post Office" sign
- "Movement Maps" created in Lesson 4
- The Mystery Letter and envelope
- List of events in "The Mystery Letter" story written on the blackboard or a large piece of butcher paper, including names of performers and narrators for each scene (See Live Action: *Living Postage Stamps.*)
- Stamp design drawings created in Lesson 13. (These may be displayed along with printed narrator descriptions for each stamp/scene from your list.)
- Other artifacts and artwork created by the students about their experiences in Lessons 1–13 (optional).

3. Plan questions and comments for each activity that will direct the attention of the audience to the effectiveness of your students' words and actions (see Commentary, below).

DAY OF PUBLIC SHARING EVENT:

1. When the visiting class arrives, welcome them as Post Office officials and introduce your class as a company of expert Stamp and Sticker Designers. Briefly describe their research on Postal Workers and their work as Postal Detectives in the case of the Mystery Letter.

2. Show any or all of the activities developed in Lessons 2, 4, 11, 12, and 13. We suggest that you make the "Living Postage Stamps" developed in Lessons 12 and 13 the final segment of your public sharing. During the sharing of these drama forms, direct the attention of your audience with comments and questions (see Commentary, below). This is also an opportunity to instruct students about the proper etiquette for being audience members.

3. After the "Living Postage Stamps" have been presented, have the adult in role as the Postmaster General come forward to congratulate the Designers and present them with their contract (see Materials / Preparation, above). Alternatively, ask someone from your school to bring the contract to the classroom, as if it has just been delivered to the school.

4. At the end of your sharing and after the contract has been presented, have your class gather in the performance area and ask the audience for comments and questions. Call on your own students to answer questions—they will enjoy being the "experts" and will have the opportunity to practice public speaking skills.

5. Describe for the visiting class any of the various items you have on display and invite your visitors to walk around your classroom examining the items. Your own students may also mill around, describing items and answering questions.

COMMENTARY:

Sharing with others can be a pleasurable learning experience if there is no pressure on students to perform. Direct the attention of your students (both audience members and presenters) to details of each segment of the presentation rather than to the performers themselves. This takes the focus off individuals while guiding students in both groups to think carefully and use their powers of observation. You can "...(make) the 'showing' part of the learning experience, so that it is seen as an element of the process, not the result...looking at other peoples' work will enable them to compare, pick up an idea or two, and perhaps discover a new perspective which will deepen the meaning for them." (Norah Morgan and Julianna Saxton, *Teaching Drama*)

With any experience of sharing/showing in this curriculum, students learn about how to be good audience members with regard to proper etiquette and intelligent observation. When you teach audience members to be discriminating viewers, you also help the presenters pay attention to details of their expression. You will want your visitors to observe how effectively your class is communicating their ideas through movement, facial expression, and words. Plan what you will ask the audience to focus on in each activity; for example, "In the next stamp, see if you can tell from the expressions on their faces what the Postal Detectives might be thinking," or, "What body parts did the performers move to show their letter-stamping machine?"

You will also be asking the audience for comments at the end of each activity. Plan to ask questions that will maintain the focus of the audience on the effect of the actions and words of your students, such as, "Were you able to hear and understand all the words spoken in the interview?"

VARIATIONS:

You may choose to invite students' parents to your public sharing event. If so, it may be best to plan an evening event, as some students may be disappointed if their own parents are not able to come during the work day. Keep the event informal and low-key so that students do not feel under pressure—remember that the purpose of the event is to *inform* parents about your drama curriculum work, not for students to perform for them.

PART V
NEW PERSPECTIVES

In this section students widen their perspectives to include not only Postal Workers and their families, but other people and places that make up a community. While using the drama skills of pantomime and improvisation, students are challenged to broaden the range of characters and settings they are able to represent through their words and actions.

In "Lesson 14: Community Roles" students use costume pieces as springboards for characterization of community members. In "Lesson 15: Community Settings," students focus on the variety of locations that make up a community, and the types of people and activities that can be found in each location.

Lesson 14
Community Roles

Costume Improvisation: *Community Interviews* (30–35 minutes)

Costume Improvisation:
Community Interviews

CONTEXT:

"Our research on U.S. Postal Workers showed us that a Postal Worker may provide assistance to many people each day. Now let's think about other workers in our community who provide services to others."

SKILLS:

Understanding and expression of character

Use and development of flexible thinking and spontaneity

MATERIALS / PREPARATION:

- Blackboard and chalk

- A box of assorted hats and other costume accessories (vests, scarves, purses, and so forth). Ideally, some of the costume pieces suggest particular community roles, for example, a firefighter's hat, a police badge, a stethoscope or doctor's lab coat, a chef's hat. It is also fine to include costume pieces that are more general so that students can use their imaginations to decide what sort of person would wear each piece. Thrift stores are excellent resources for costume accessories. You can also ask the parents of your students to donate such items.

- Chairs arranged in a horseshoe facing the blackboard, with one seat in the center facing the other chairs.

PROCEDURE:

1. Ask students to name as many community workers as they can think of. Write their answers on the blackboard. Possible answers include:

firefighter	librarian
policeman or woman	grocery store checker
doctor	bus driver
restaurant worker	mom or dad, and so on
teacher	

Be sure to steer students away from gender stereotypes, reminding them, for example, that a police officer can be either a woman or a man. Also emphasize that some important roles in the community are not paid jobs. For example, moms and dads are important community workers.

2. Show students the box of costume pieces. Tell them that each costume piece will represent someone who serves the community. Explain the following procedure:

   • You will choose one volunteer, who will select a costume piece from the box, put it on, and sit in the chair at the center of the circle.

   • The student in the center will take a moment to decide what person in the community might wear the costume piece he has chosen. The student will say "Ready" when he is ready to be interviewed as that member of the community.

   • You will call on volunteers who wish to ask the community worker a question. Each student may ask one question. Possible questions might be:

   "What is your name?"
   "What is your job?"
   "Do you have any children?"
   "How long have you and your family lived in this city?"
   "What do you like to do when you get home from work?"
   "What do you like best about your job?" and so on

(Note: At this point in explaining the procedure you may want to take a few minutes to brainstorm possible questions with your students. Questions could be about such things as the community worker's job, family, hobbies, or history.)

- The student in the center will answer each question, improvising an answer that might be given by the community worker they represent. If they choose not to answer a particular question, they may say "Pass."

- After the student has had a reasonable turn (no more than 1–2 minutes) she will put the costume piece back in the box and resume her place in the circle.

- You will call on a new volunteer and the process will be repeated.

3. Do the procedure in Step 2, giving turns to as many students as desire one, or as many students as you have time for (this activity can always be repeated at another time to give all students an opportunity to be interviewed).

COMMENTARY:

This activity requires students to improvise answers in the character of a community worker. It is important to point out that there are no "right" or "wrong" answers to interview questions, as long as the interviewee is making a sincere effort to answer as their character might. If students begin giving silly answers out of self-consciousness or a desire to entertain their classmates, remind them that their job in this activity is to believe, if only for a minute or two, that they are the person who would wear that article of clothing. It is fine for them to let their character have a sense of humor, but not for the student to undermine the intent of the activity.

This activity provides students with a new perspective on interviews, as they now have an opportunity to interview someone as they were interviewed in "Lesson 11: TV Interview." As your students are not likely to be experienced in interview techniques, it will be helpful to provide them with sample questions as well as have them brainstorm possible questions before beginning to interview each other (see Step 2). Just as the interviewees must make an effort to believe fully in their characters, the student interviewers should also be encouraged to think seriously about their role.

VARIATIONS:

Wearing costume pieces is enjoyable for students and will greatly aid them in "getting the feel" of a character. If you are not able to obtain costume pieces, however, you can do this activity by writing the names of community workers on cards. It will also be helpful to include pictures or symbols on the cards to help students decode the words. Have volunteers choose a card that interests them, then be interviewed as the community worker on the card.

Use this activity in a literature lesson by having the student in the center be a character in a story that everyone in your class is familiar with. Student interviewers can then ask questions pertaining to the story. The following questions are examples of what interviewers might ask a student playing Goldilocks from the story "Goldilocks and the Three Bears":

"Why did you decide to go into the bears' house?"
"Were you scared when you woke up and saw the bears?"
"What did you tell your parents when you got home?"

Lesson 15
Community Settings

Improvisation & Pantomime: *Community Museum* (35–40min.)

Improvisation & Pantomime: *Community Museum*

CONTEXT:
"Today we'll create a 'Living Museum' where visitors come to see some different places that make up a community."

SKILLS:
Understanding and expression of setting
Artistic collaboration

MATERIALS / PREPARATION:
- Blackboard and chalk

- You will need 4-5 areas of your classroom where small groups of students can create "exhibits" of different places in the community. You may choose to rearrange your classroom furniture to make more space available for these exhibits.

- A bell, drum, or other auditory signal (or you can simply flick the light switch in Step 7 of the Procedure)

PROCEDURE:
1. Tell students that the class will be creating a "Living Museum" that will show various places in a community. The museum will consist of four or five exhibits that visitors can walk through, each showing a different place in the community—what kind of people one might find there, and what kinds of activities take

---

place there. Each exhibit will be confined to a specific area of the classroom.

2. Ask students to name some community places they might want to show in their museum, writing their ideas on the blackboard as they speak. Your completed list might include the following:
   library
   grocery store
   doctor's office
   gas station
   bank
   Post Office
   community park
   police station

3. Ask for a student volunteer to choose one of the places listed on the board that he would like to re-create as a museum exhibit. Ask that volunteer to decide where in the classroom he would like the exhibit to be, and to go there. Ask the student to decide on an activity someone might do in that place, then begin to do the activity in pantomime. For example, a student might choose to create a gas station exhibit by going to a corner of the room and showing, in pantomime, that she is filling her car with gas.

4. Choose three or four more volunteers who would like to help create the exhibit initiated in Step 3. Ask those volunteers to join the first student in pantomiming additional activities that would take place in that location. In the gas station example, additional students might wash their windshields, go to the cashier to pay for gas, or put air in their tires. One student might choose to play the cashier.

5. Tell your class that you will now help the rest of them organize other community exhibits. Before proceeding, clarify that each group will need to decide:

   • What role each person will play in the setting (such as a customer, someone who works in that setting, and so on)

- Why each person is in the setting and what activity they are doing there

- How the physical setting will be arranged. Students can use some of the furniture and other items in the classroom to create their exhibits. In the gas station example, students might decide to have three chairs be the gas pumps and a table be the cashier's counter. Encourage groups to create believable portrayals of their community settings and to think about what details and actions they could include to make their exhibit look realistic.

Repeat Steps 3 and 4 with the rest of the class, organizing them into groups exhibit by exhibit. Meanwhile, the first group may continue working together to organize their exhibit, as needed. Alternatively, you may ask the first group to take their seats so that the whole class watches while you work with each group in turn.

6. Once students have organized their exhibits, call the class's attention to one of the exhibits. Allow the students in that group to show their setting in action for approximately one minute while the rest of the groups watch from their places. Students may pantomime in silence or speak dialogue if they choose as they move in their roles in the setting they have chosen to create. After each group has shown their exhibit, allow the performers to explain or comment on their actions if they choose. Repeat this procedure with each exhibit.

7. Tell students that when you ring a bell (or other signal) the museum will be open for visitors and that one person at a time from each group will have a chance to walk through the museum. Choose one student from each group to be a "visitor." The visitors will walk from location to location as the performers show the activities in their exhibits. The visitors may move from exhibit to exhibit as a group, or each individual may move through the museum at his own pace. The performers may show their activities in silence or speak as they choose.

Ring the bell and allow the visiting group to walk through the museum for approximately 1–2 minutes. Ring the bell again to "close" the museum, then choose a new group of visitors, one from each exhibit. Repeat until all students have had a turn as museum visitors.

COMMENTARY:

The goal of this activity is to create a realistic, believable setting through physical action. Encourage students to concentrate on the details of what their character would be doing in the setting. For example, at the library exhibit the student playing the librarian might pantomime stamping dates in books or typing requests for information into the computer. The students playing parents at the library might pull imaginary books from shelves and look at them to find a book their child would enjoy. Those playing other library patrons might pantomime copying information from encyclopedias into their notebooks.

Some students may be anxious to "make something happen" in their scene, such as an argument in the library or a robber coming into the grocery store. In drama improvisation this is known as "playwriting." Although playwriting in improvisations is a creative and worthwhile activity, it is not the goal of this lesson (creating a believable setting through physical action). Encourage students to concentrate on the details of their actions in the setting rather than rushing to create dramatic conflict.

VARIATIONS:

Invite a group of students from another classroom, or your students' parents, to visit your community museum. Prepare for the event by having each group of students create a sign to label their exhibit. Allow the visitors to wander through your museum as students perform actions in their community settings.

Adapt this activity to another context by choosing different categories of settings for a museum. You might have students create a sports and recreation museum, a habitat museum, or a world cultures museum. Students could also create museums with fanciful settings such as an outer space museum or a fairy tale museum.

PART VI
DRAMA AND LITERATURE

Drama and literature share the common goal of communication. Literature is dramatic action captured in the printed word, drama is literature come to life. By exploring literature selections through drama, students gain a first-hand experience of the power and purpose of the written word.

By bringing stories and poetry into action, young students begin to understand that words are symbols that hold the key to a world of ideas, events, and feelings. According to Betty Jane Wagner in *Dorothy Heathcote / Drama as a Learning Medium*, "A reader who has discovered what words on a page actually are—distilled human experience—has cracked the code forever. Such a person can translate any text into meaning by bringing to it the understanding, first, that it is indeed a code to be cracked, a script to be interpreted, not for an audience, but for one's own illumination; and, second, that to make sense of it requires the application of one's own experience."

Through drama, students are exposed to and come to appreciate literature of many kinds, including poetry and rhyme, folktales and fairy tales, fables and myths, and contemporary children's books, as well as literature written specifically for the theater. Some nonfiction materials, including biographies, also hold rich possibilities for dramatic experience. In becoming personally involved in each selection, students internalize its structure, enriching their skills as future composers of language as well as interpreters of it.

As students have moved through *Mail and Mystery, Family and Friends,* they have been moving from drama generated by and for themselves toward drama that interprets the words of others. The focus of the lessons in the following section, however, is still on the student's own experience rather than on creating an experience for an outside audience. Although dramatizations of many of the stories and poems may certainly be shared with others, the primary goal is still to encourage students to feel and express belief in an imaginary situation—here, the event in a piece of literature.

In this section of the curriculum, students will be guided to respond to written selections in several ways, including through movement and pantomime, poetry, and dramatizing stories with action and dialogue. Each lesson will model one type of response using a specific literature selection, the text of which is included in the lesson. Other selections that can be explored using the same procedure are suggested at the end of each lesson. You are, of course also welcome to use favorite literature selections of your own.

Exploring literature through drama provides students with opportunities to express and create, to collaborate with others, and to gain a lifelong appreciation for the world of language.

Lesson 16
Literature and Movement
Neither Rain, nor Sleet… A Mail Carrier's Adventure (5–8 min.)

LITERATURE AND MOVEMENT:

"Neither Rain, nor Sleet…" by Pamela Gerke is an example of a Movement Story—a story that is narrated by the teacher as the students move spontaneously. In a Movement Story students play each of the characters, switching from one character to another as the narration dictates. The purpose of a Movement Story is to encourage full-body expressiveness through pantomime and dance. Movement Stories represent the combining of creative dance and drama.

Neither Rain, nor Sleet… A Mail Carrier's Adventure

CONTEXT:
"Today we're going to move to a poem about a Mail Carrier's working day, traveling from one place to another delivering the mail."

SKILLS:
Use of the whole body in movement
Expressive use of body and movement

MATERIALS / PREPARATION:
- Ideally, when you tell this story to your class, you should do the movements along with your students (we encourage teachers to always participate in movement activities). We recommend that you do one of the following:

  – Photocopy the text, so that it can be easily held in one hand.
  – Write the story in large letters on a big piece of paper that you tape to the wall. (This last option will also allow students to

---

see the correspondence between the written and spoken words and the movements.)

- (Optional) Tape or CD player and a tape or CD of light, "floating" instrumental music, such as a recording of "Spring Song" by Felix Mendelssohn

- Plenty of movement space in the room

PROCEDURE:

1. Tell students that they will be following a mail carrier's route on a typical working day. This is a Movement Story, meaning that students will do the movements and pantomimes as you narrate the story, which is written as a rhyming poem.

2. Ask students if anyone knows what a motto is and briefly discuss the definition of this word. Read the Mail Carriers' Motto at the beginning of the poem to students. Ask them to say it with you a few times, to build memory. Tell students that when this Motto occurs in the story, they may say it aloud with you.

3. Ask students to find an empty spot to stand where they can stretch their arms without touching another person. Tell students that during some parts of the story they will move while staying in one spot (Self Space), while other parts of the story will require them to move around the room (General Space). Tell students that they will be moving in different directions (forward, backwards, and sideways) and on different levels (low, medium, and high).

4. Read the following story while doing the movements described on the right in italics. Pause as often as needed while maintaining the rhythm of the poem. When desired, interject comments and suggestions in order to keep your students focused or to make observations about their movements.

"Neither Rain, nor Sleet..."
A Mail Carrier's Route
by Pamela Gerke

Mail Carriers are we
And this our motto be:

"Neither rain, nor sleet,   *students say motto with you*
Nor dark of night
Shall stay these couriers
From their flight."

First we walk from house to house   *walk forward around the room*
Moving forward on our feet
But when a growling dog appears,   *stop*
Tiptoe backwards down the street.   *tiptoe backwards*

Dog danger has passed—
Walk forward once more   *walk forward around the room*
Delivering mail
From door-to-door.   *mime delivering mail*

And when moving forward becomes a bore:
Walk sideways for a change.
Walk to the right...   *walk sideways, to the right*
Now to the left...   *walk sideways to the left*
(People will think we are strange!)   *(It's not crucial that students
know right from left—simply
encourage them to move
sideways in both directions.)*

Now, when out delivering mail   *stop*
It happens sooner or later
That we come to a tall building
And must take the elevator.

Enter at Level Number One	*crouch low*
Push the button / close the door	*mime pushing button*
And as we rise from 1 to 5	
Let's count every floor:	
1–2–3–4–5	*while slowly counting aloud, rise up to tiptoes*
"Here's your mail—see you later!"	*mime giving mail to someone*
Down we go in the elevator:	
5–4–3–2–1	*while slowly counting aloud, sink down to crouch*
There's mail for the basement,	
We must keep going down.	*sink down to lie with stomach on floor*
Alas! The basement's flooded!	
We must swim or else we'll drown!	*stomach on floor, do swimming motions with arms, legs, breath, etc.*
"Here's your mail—see you later!"	*mime giving mail to someone*
Up we go in the elevator.	*slowly stand up*
Now walk out the door	*walk forward*
And out to the street—	
A parade is coming!	
Let's march to the beat.	*march around the room for several seconds and then stop*
We marched to the beat of the band,	
And now we've come to a stop.	*(students should also stop)*
A circus clown	
Spins us 'round and 'round...	*standing in place, slowly spin around, with arms out*
'Til we arrive at the circus Big Top!	*to sides stop*
Letter for an acrobat—	*mime holding up a letter*

We *must* deliver it!   *mime walking*
Across the tightrope, carefully...   *forward on a tightrope*
"Here's your mail—no time to visit!"   *mime giving mail to someone*

Backwards now,   *mime walking backwards on*
Without turning 'round,   *a tightrope*
And whatever you do:
DON'T LOOK DOWN!!!

Now grab the trapeze: *mime holding trapeze bar*
Swing low, swing high...   *high overhead swing arms*
                                          and body from one side to
                                          another, high / low / high

Swing again...   *repeat, reversing direction*
                                          of movement

And then,   *stop*
Into the safety net we'll fly!   *fall gently to the floor*

No broken bones...   *squeeze arms and legs*
                                          with hands

On our feet again—   *stand up*
Now off to the forest we go!   *walk forward around the room*
Our arms must reach high   *reach up arms*
To swing on the vines   *mime swinging on vines,*
                                          arm over arm

Bringing mail to the apes, you know.

"Postcard from Tarzan!"   *mime giving letter to someone*
HELP!!! We're caught in quicksand!

Slowly sinking down, down,   *slowly sink down to floor*
Sucked in a slimy funnel...

But we *must* never fail   *(in a somewhat desperate voice)*
To deliver the mail
So we escape through an   *crawl forward, either on*
underground tunnel...   *stomach or on hands*
     and knees

At the end of the tunnel
We stop and we find   *stop*
An old, shaky ladder—
Up, up we climb...   *slowly rise to standing while*
     miming climbing up a
     shaky ladder

Here's a hot air balloon—
Get in / *up* we drift   *mime climbing into balloon*
     basket, rise

Floating higher and higher...   *up on tiptoes and gently*
     "float" around the room

To a nest in the cliffs.   *(optional:) Turn on "floating"*
     music. Play for 30 seconds or
     more while students float
     freely on tiptoes around
     the room.

     When ready, turn off the music.

Mail for the eagles   *mime giving mail to someone*
On a lofty mountain peak—
What's this?!! A *hole* in our balloon!
It's starting to leak!

Grab a parachute and JUMP!!!   *mime putting on a parachute*
and *jump*...Land with a bump.   *fall gently to the floor*

We crawl home exhausted,   *crawl forward, either on*
     stomach or on hands
     and knees

| Eat dinner, climb in bed | *mime eating, then lying down in bed* |

And dream of clowns and quicksand,
While our Motto runs through our heads:

"Neither rain, nor sleet	*speak together, in a*
Nor dark of night	*dreamy voice*
Shall stay these couriers	
From their flight."	

Goodnight!

The End

COMMENTARY:

Movement Stories guide students in developing body awareness and in exploring movement possibilities (see *Movement Stories For Children* by Landalf and Gerke and other movement-related books in Bibliography). Movement Stories center around specific movement concepts; "Neither Rain, nor Sleet..." emphasizes the concepts of direction and level.

In movement, direction (forward, backwards, right, left, sideways, up, down) is determined by the surface of the body that is leading us through space. Direction is differentiated from "facing," which is determined by one's place in the room. For example, one can face forward yet move in the direction "backwards" (being led by the back of one's body). Level (low, middle, high) determines whether we are close to the ground or far away. *Rising* is moving from a low level to a high level; *sinking* is moving from a high level to a low level.

It is helpful to practice this poem before presenting it so that you can speak each verse with a steady meter—students will respond to its rhythm. Feel free to stop between each verse and allow time for students to move. At these times you can make observations about students' movements, such as, "I notice Helen is rising very swiftly to a high level." Or, "I see Pam uses her arms to balance herself on the tightrope."

VARIATIONS:

You can add other recorded music segments to various sections of this poem and allow students to dance freely while the music plays for a minute or so. Play a Sousa march during the marching band section or circus-type music during the Big Top section.

You can further explore rhyming poetry and movement by creating a rhyming poem together. Give students one word, such as *clown,* and ask for suggestions of rhyming words, such as *frown, town* and *around.* Write their words on the blackboard and when you have several, use them to make up a little poem with your class; for example: "The clown / with a frown / came to town / and rolled around." Speak the poem aloud slowly while students improvise movement to it.

Lesson 17
Poetry & Movement

Creative Writing & Movement: *Family Poem* (25–30 minutes)

Creative Writing & Movement
Family Poem

CONTEXT:

"Let's use our observations about the family lives of Postal Workers to write a poem about families and do movement with it."

SKILLS:

Expressive use of body and movement
Artistic collaboration

MATERIALS / PREPARATION:

- Blackboard and chalk
- The following written on the blackboard:

    Families

    _____

    _____

    _____

    _____

    _____

    Families

PROCEDURE:

1. Tell students that together you will write a poem about families by deciding on one word to put on each blank line. The words must either:

   • Describe families (adjectives, i.e., warm, busy, crowded).

   • Tell something that families do (verb ending in "ing," i.e., working, playing, arguing).

   Ask students to raise their hands to suggest words for their poem. Write students' ideas on one side of the blackboard, but do not fill in the blank lines of the poem yet. Be aware that not all of your students have families and that some may have unhappy family lives; therefore, it is possible that some "uncomfortable" words may be suggested. It is important to acknowledge all points of view by writing every student's suggestion on the board.

2. Have students decide, by voting or by general consensus, which five of the suggested words they would like to use to fill in the blank lines of the poem. In guiding students to make this choice you might emphasize choosing words that suggest action, as the poem will be used to create a sequence of movements. You can also encourage a choice of words that show variety and contrast in describing families. (For example, a poem could include words that express feelings about families, describe work activities and describe recreational activities rather than consist of words from only one of these categories.) Write the five words the students select on the blank lines of the poem. The finished poem might look something like this (this is only an example):

   Families
   Warm
   Busy
   Cleaning
   Arguing
   Playing baseball
   Families

3. Ask students for ideas of how they can show each line of the poem in movement. Beside each line of the poem write a short phrase describing how the students have decided to interpret that line in movement. The example above might be interpreted in this way:

Families
students pose together in groups of 4 or 5, as in a family photo

Warm
each "family" huddles close together

Busy
family groups break apart and students walk briskly around the room

Cleaning
each student mimes a household cleaning job such as sweeping, scrubbing the floor or washing dishes

Arguing
all students come together and mime arguing with each other

Playing baseball
each student mimes some aspect of playing baseball such as throwing or catching a ball or swinging a bat

Families
students pose once again in their original groups

(Note: The phrases you write on the blackboard describing movement can be much shorter and simpler than the descriptions above as they will simply serve as memory aids for the students. We have included detailed descriptions here to give you some examples of the types of movements that can be used in this activity.)

4. Say the poem aloud as students do the movements they have chosen for each word. Be sure to say the poem slowly enough so that students have adequate time to perform each movement and to transition from one movement to the next without rushing. Do the movements along with the students to provide them with a model of full, active participation.

5. Divide the class in half, assigning one half to be performers and the other half to be the audience members. Say the poem aloud again as the performers do the actions while the audience members watch. Afterwards, ask audience members to comment on what they saw. Guide their comments by asking questions such as:

"What was your favorite part of the poem to watch? What were you thinking about as you watched that part?"

"What did they do that made it seem like they were really playing baseball?"

"Could you tell by the expressions on their faces how they felt about doing housework?" and so on.

6. Reverse roles and repeat.

COMMENTARY:

This activity gives students a chance to synthesize some of their experiences about family relationships from earlier lessons in this curriculum. It also provides an opportunity for them to combine both literal and abstract movement in interpreting language. The fact that the students generate both the words and movements for the poem gives them a chance to be creative as both linguistic and kinesthetic artists.

It is important to be aware that some of your students may experience difficulties in their family lives that may be reflected in their choice of words for this poem. If one of your students suggests a word that connotes separation, violence, or another family disturbance, it is up to you, as teacher, to determine whether the suggestion is one that can be handled by your students with physical and emotional safety. Under no circumstances, however, should a student be made to feel that her suggestion is "wrong." Drama can provide a safe outlet for strong feelings; difficult issues should be dealt with as sensitively, yet honestly, as possible.

VARIATIONS:

After creating movement to the poem as a whole class, divide students into groups of four or five and allow each group to create their own movement interpretations of the words. The groups may either use the poem generated by the class or write a new poem of their own.

Use this Procedure to create poems with movement on other subjects such as feelings, colors, elements of nature, or elements of city life.

Lesson 18
Tableaux and Story Illustrations
Tableaux and Story Creation: *Living Picture Book* (30–35 min.)

TABLEAUX AND LITERATURE:

The drama form of tableaux can be used to interpret illustrations from children's books. Creating tableaux based on illustrations aids students in seeing the possible connections between the characters, setting, and plot of a story. Bringing to life alternative scenes suggested by the illustrations gives students the opportunity to act as authors of their own story.

Tableaux and Story Creation:
Living Picture Book

CONTEXT:

"Just as we used our bodies to show family photographs and stamp designs, we can also use them to show illustrations from a story. Today I will be showing you illustrations from a book about a community of people who learn the hard way that it doesn't pay to be greedy."

SKILLS:

Use and development of powers of observation and awareness of details
Use and development of imagination and creativity
Development of discriminating perception as an audience member

MATERIALS / PREPARATION:

- A copy of the children's book *Why the Sky is Far Away,* a Nigerian folktale retold by Mary-Joan Gerson and illustrated by Carla Golembe, available in many libraries and bookstores. If you are unable to obtain this book or if your students are already familiar with the story, you may present this lesson using any children's

---

book that has expressive, vivid illustrations and a story that is unfamiliar to your students.

- You will need a performing area that can accommodate up to 15 students in tableau and an audience area for the rest of the class.

PROCEDURE:

1. Choose one illustration from *Why the Sky is Far Away* and show it to your students, making sure that all of them can see it clearly. Discuss the illustration with your students by asking questions such as the following:

   - Who might the people in this picture be? (Allow students to discuss each character in the illustration.)

   - What do you think might be happening in this picture?

   - Where do you think these characters are?

   - If this picture were to come to life, what might each character do or say?

   As students have not yet heard the story, they will be generating their own ideas of what might be happening in the illustration, which may be completely different from the actual scene in the story that the illustration depicts.

2. Using ideas generated in the discussion above, facilitate the students in deciding which of the ideas they would like to try out as they make the illustration "come to life." Solidify their decision by repeating it back to them, for example (referring to the illustration on pages 12 and 13):

   "The man with the stick is the king. He's mad at the people and he's telling them to go away. The person holding the umbrella is his servant. The people in the front of the picture are listening to a sad letter the woman is reading. The person pointing up is looking at the clouds because it looks like it might rain. The people are in a little village with huts.

If the scene came to life the king would yell at the people walk-ing and they would walk away. The woman would read the letter out loud and the person next to her would cry. The person pointing up would say 'Look, it's about to rain!!'"

3. Ask for student volunteers to come to the performing area to create a "living illustration." Choose one volunteer to play each character in the illustration. You can select additional students to represent trees, huts, or other nonhuman elements in the pic-ture. Have the student volunteers work together to create a replica of the illustration. The tableau should ideally include all the elements in the actual illustration. Audience members may help them by making suggestions such as *"The king should be on this side of the road."* Or *"Maybe Bobby and Cheryle could make a hut together."*

4. When the illustration has been organized to the students' satis-faction, have the performers freeze in their positions. Tell them that when you clap your hands (or give another signal such as ringing a bell) the illustration will "come to life," and each char-acter will move or speak to show the scene the class has described. Clap your hands and allow the scene to come to life in action and dialogue for approximately 30 seconds. Say "Freeze" to stop the action (students do not have to return to their original positions).

5. Have the entire class briefly discuss the scene. Ask questions that focus the audience on the dialogue and action in the scene and how effectively the ideas of the group were communicated by the performers. Also allow the performers to comment on the thoughts, actions, and dialogue of their characters in the scene.

6. Repeat the above procedure with three or four more illustra-tions, choosing new student volunteers each time. Make sure that all students who wish to participate in creating a tableau have an opportunity to do so.

7. Conclude the lesson by reading aloud the story *Why the Sky is Far Away*. Discuss with the students how the story is similar to or different from the ideas they suggested.

COMMENTARY:
This lesson approaches the creation of tableaux by students in a different way than have previous lessons in this curriculum. Rather than creating their own scenes from a wide range of possibilities as they did in "Family Photo Album" (Lesson 5) or "Living Postage Stamps" (Lessons 12 and 13), in this lesson students are asked to use their powers of observation to replicate an already existing depiction. In contrast to the structure of having to re-create an illustration accurately, the other goal of this activity is to encourage imagination and creativity by having students interpret the illustration in their own way as they bring it to life.

Although a limited number of students can participate at once in the actual creation of each tableau, in this lesson the audience members are also involved in story creation and scene direction. Allow the audience to be as active as possible in helping the performers create the tableau and in making decisions about what will happen when the scene comes to life.

VARIATIONS:
Do this activity using an illustrated story that is familiar to your students, or read an illustrated story aloud before having students depict the illustrations. In this variation the scene will "come to life" as it actually does in the author's version of the story.

Do this activity using reproductions of famous paintings. Discuss what might be happening in the painting, have students re-create the painting as a tableau, then let the tableau come to life, showing the students' interpretation of the work of art.

ALTERNATE SELECTION FOR
STORY ILLUSTRATIONS AND TABLEAUX:
The Flame of Peace: A Tale of the Aztecs by Deborah Nourse Lattimore has numerous colorful illustrations in an Aztec style.

Though students may need some guidance in identifying the elements in the stylized illustrations, they will enjoy interpreting the unique characters and settings.

Follow the Drinking Gourd by Jeanette Winters is the illustrated story of a slave family escaping to freedom on the Underground Railroad. The simple illustrations can be easily depicted as tableaux, and can be interpreted in numerous ways. In addition, reading the story aloud to students will provide them with information on an important segment of American history.

Lesson 19
Literature and Dramatization

Story Dramatization: *A Stone in the Road* (40 minutes)

LITERATURE AND DRAMATIZATION:

Dramatizing a story is one of the most exciting and satisfying ways for children to experience literature. In dramatizing a story, students make it their own by improvising action and dialogue within the structure of a tale. Experiencing a story through drama allows children to emphasize the aspects of the story that they find most compelling. The fact that the actions and dialogue are improvised on the spot, rather than preplanned and rehearsed, reduces the anxiety that may be present when memorization is required and thus allows students to become more fully involved in the story. Although a story dramatization may be performed for an audience, the emphasis of this activity remains on the experience of the participants.

Story Dramatization: *A Stone in the Road*

CONTEXT:
"Today you'll hear and act out the story of how the people in a community were taught a lesson about helping one another."

SKILLS:
Understanding and expression of character
Communication with an audience

MATERIALS / PREPARATION:
- A large box to represent the stone—must be sturdy enough for students to sit on. Alternatively, use a chair to represent the stone.

- A cloth bag with real or pretend coins in it
- Familiarize yourself with the text of "The Stone in the Road," included in this lesson. You may either tell the story in your own words or read it aloud.

PROCEDURE:

1. Tell students that they will be hearing a story about how one member of a community set an example for his neighbors. Ask them to listen to find out what this man did.

2. Tell or read aloud "The Stone in the Road."

3. Discuss the story by asking students the following questions:
   - Who are the characters in this story?
   - How did the story begin? How did it end?
   - What part of the story was most interesting to you?
   - What other people in the village might have come down the road?

4. Tell the students they will now have a chance to act out the story of "The Stone in the Road." As a group, decide where the locations in the story will be in your drama space: Where will the road be? Which direction will villagers travel to get to the market? Where will the Duke place the stone? Where are the bushes that the Duke will hide in? Show students the box or chair that will be used to represent the stone, and the bag of coins. Allow students to place other props or furniture pieces, as needed, to represent objects or locations in the story (see Commentary).

5. Discuss with students what characters will be included in their dramatization of the story. Choose volunteers to play the Duke, Farmer, Egg sellers, Children and the Young Man. The gender of any role may be changed. (For example, the Duke can be a Duchess and the Young Man can be a Young Woman.) The rest of the students will play other villagers who interact with the stone.

6. Ask all students to make these decisions about their characters:

- *Who* is my character (Am I a farmer, a peddler, mother, child, and so on.)
- *Where* am I going? (Am I going to market, to visit a sick friend, and so forth.)
- *What* will I do or say when I see the stone?
- *Where* will my character be when the story begins?

7. Ask students to get into the places their characters would be at the beginning of the story. Guide students in acting out the story, allowing them to create their own action and dialogue as much as possible. Be available as the narrator of the story to help guide the dramatization as needed, making statements such as *"A Farmer came down the road"* to signal a student to enter, or *"The Duke looked at the Young Man and said…"* to encourage dialogue. Make your narration as minimal as possible, using it only to give the dramatization structure or to help a performer who is unsure of what to do or say.

8. Play the story once again with different students playing the various roles. This time students will be more familiar with the story and more able to recreate it fully without your guidance.

9. Divide the group in half and have half the students act out the story with the other half as audience. Afterwards, ask the audience questions that guide them in evaluating the expressive qualities of the performers and their own experience of the dramatization. For example: *"What did Aaron do to make us believe he was the Duke?'* *"How could we tell that Jenny and Rita were carrying eggs?"* *"How did John show us that seeing the stone in the road made him angry?"* *"What was the most exciting part of the story for you?"* Monitor the students' responses to make sure they provide positive feedback for the performers. Focus the evaluation on how effectively the performers presented the story rather than on the shortcomings of particular performers.

10. Switch performers and audience members and repeat.

A Stone in the Road
a traditional tale retold by Helen Landalf

Once upon a time, in a lovely country village, there lived a rich but generous Duke. The Duke loved the people who lived in the village and was always willing to lend a hand to help anyone in need.

As the years went by, however, the Duke noticed that the people of the village were becoming lazier and lazier. No one seemed to want to go out of their way to help a friend or a neighbor, depending instead on the Duke to provide assistance. So the Duke thought of a clever plan: One morning before anyone in the village had awakened, he pushed and pulled a huge stone right into the middle of the village road where it would be in everyone's way. Before he set the stone in place, he took a small bag of gold and placed it in the road. Then he settled the heavy stone right on top of the bag of gold.

"Now I will hide in the bushes and watch," said the Duke. "From there I can see if anyone will be willing to move the stone out of the way so that the people of the village can go about their business." And hide in the bushes he did.

As the morning sun rose, the people of the village began to wake up and start their day's work. The first person to come down the road was a farmer with a wagon load of hay. When he got to the stone, he kicked it and said, "What in the world is this stone doing in the middle of the road? Well, I won't be the one to move it, that's for sure!" So he drove his wagon around the stone and went off to market.

Next to reach the stone were two women carrying baskets of eggs to sell at the market. "Who on earth put this stone here!" exclaimed one woman. Her friend replied, "I don't know, but I wish that whoever put it here would take it away." As she spoke she sat down on the stone for a short rest and a snack. After a few moments the two women continued down the road.

A minute later three children came skipping down the road. "Look at this stone—it's right in everyone's way!" they cried. "The Duke should get his men to move it," one of them suggested. Then the children decided that the stone was perfect for playing leapfrog, so they spent a few minutes taking turns jumping over the stone, then skipped on their way.

All day the Duke watched from his hiding place and all day he saw many people come to the stone—mothers and fathers, children and elders, rich people and beggars. Each person who saw it said something about the stone and many used it as a resting place or a table, a hitching post or a stage. But no one lifted a hand to move the stone that was in everyone's way.

Finally, toward evening, a young man came along. Now, this young man came from a very poor family and he was always hungry. Nevertheless, when he saw the stone he said, "Why, this stone is in everyone's way. I will move it so that people can travel easily down the road." So the young man pushed, pulled, and shoved until he had moved the stone out of the road. Only then did he see the bag of gold that the Duke had hidden underneath.

"What's this!" exclaimed the young man. "Oh dear, I must find who this bag of gold belongs to."

"My boy, that gold belongs to you," proclaimed the Duke as he climbed out of his hiding place. "It is your reward for being willing to go out of your way to help others. Take it and buy food and presents for your family. You will never be hungry again."

But, as the young man was a very generous fellow, he wanted to use some of the gold to make his friends and neighbors happy. So he invited everyone in the village to a huge feast where they ate and drank, sang, and danced all night long. After that, whenever someone needed help or there was a job to be done everyone in the village came running to help. "Remember the stone in the road," they would say.

COMMENTARY:

This story is an excellent one for giving students an opportunity to create actions for their characters. Each character's actions will have a definite structure (approach the stone, interact with the stone, leave the stone), but within that structure there is plenty of room for students to be creative. For example, one student might decide to have her character sit on the stone, another to yell at it, another to lie on it for a nap.

When performing this story for an audience of classmates, encourage students to speak loudly enough for the audience to hear, and to position themselves so that they can be seen by the audience. Sharing a story with an audience gives students a reason to "project their voices" and face the audience as they speak.

Students enjoy the fun of creating their own sets and props from furniture and other objects in the classroom. The addition of sets and props to a dramatization helps students feel that they are truly "putting on a play." Keep sets and props to a minimum, however, or students will become distracted by them and diverted from the point of the lesson, which is to recreate a story in action and dialogue.

VARIATIONS:

After dramatizing the story as written, ask students to discuss how they might change the ending of the story. Perhaps they will decide that the young man (or woman) moves the stone, but the bag of gold has disappeared. Or they might decide that the whole village bands together to move the stone, then shares (or fights over) the bag of gold. Have students dramatize the story again with the new ending they have created.

Have the students make a backdrop for the story by drawing or painting a mural of a rural village and a road on a large piece of butcher paper or on the blackboard. Several students could work together to make a papier-mâché stone.

**OTHER SELECTIONS FOR
LITERATURE AND DRAMATIZATION:**
Many traditional tales and folk tales may be dramatized by children. Virginia Haviland has retold tales of many countries in her *Favorite Fairy Tales* series (see Bibliography). Excellent stories for dramatization can also be found in Winifred Ward's *Stories to Dramatize* (see Bibliography).

Lesson 20
Story Dramatization /
Changing Elements

The Boy Who Cried Wolf (20–25 minutes)

This lesson combines interpretive and generative artistry: Students interpret a known story while generating ideas for changing it. By changing the basic elements of character, setting, or time period, students both define what these elements are and understand how they effect each other and the overall story. The literature selection is a traditional fable that will be familiar to many students and that has a moral relevant to living in a community with others.

The Boy Who Cried Wolf

CONTEXT:
"One of the important values to remember when living with others in a community is to always tell the truth."

SKILLS:
Understanding and expression of character and setting
Artistic collaboration

MATERIALS / PREPARATION:
- Arrange your space so that one area can be "the village" and another area can be "the meadow" where the Boy watches his sheep, with space to travel between the two areas.

- Familiarize yourself with the text of "The Boy Who Cried Wolf," included in this lesson. You may either tell the story in your own words or read it aloud.

PROCEDURE:

1. Tell students that they will dramatize an old story called a fable. Fables are short and simple traditional stories that have a moral, a lesson to be learned. This particular fable tells about the people in a community and how they reacted to a certain boy and his prank.

2. Tell or read aloud the story "The Boy Who Cried Wolf."

3. Lead students in a short discussion of the story, including a discussion about its moral. Ask students questions such as:

   "What is the moral or lesson of the story?"

   "Do you think the boy learned this lesson in the end?"

   "Why did the boy decide to play his trick?"

   "How do you think he felt when the villagers refused to help him at the end?"

   "What might have happened to his sheep in the end?"

   "What are some of the things the villagers might have been doing when they heard the boy cry, 'Wolf'?"

   "What do you think the villagers thought the first time they heard him cry, 'Wolf'? The second time? The third?" (and so on)

4. Ask for a volunteer to play the Boy. The rest of the class will play the Villagers. (Alternatively, you can have half or one-third of your class dramatize the story while the other half watches, and then have them switch roles.) Some students may also want to play the Wolf and the Sheep—this is fine but if they do, we recommend that you have them play the "Wolf attack" scene in slow motion.

   Ask each of the students who are playing the Villagers to decide what jobs they are doing in the village when the Boy cries "Wolf!" Possible jobs include: selling things in a store, taking care of a baby, weeding the garden, and so forth.

Show students where the village and meadow areas are in your room, and the route between the two. To begin the dramatization, the Villagers could be in the village, pantomiming doing chores, and the Boy could be in the meadow with the sheep.

5. Improvise a dramatization of the story. You can add narration as needed, but also allow students to improvise dialogue. If you've split the class in half or thirds, have the performing group switch places with the audience group and repeat the dramatization.

6. After students have dramatized the story as written, tell them that it's possible to change some of the basic elements of a fable without essentially changing the story or its moral. Define for students the elements they may change—characters, setting (location) or time period (see below)—and ask them to describe these elements in the original fable.

Now repeat the dramatization several times; but each time, before you begin, decide with your class which element(s) to change and what the change(s) will be. The story is short enough that you should be able to dramatize it several times. Each time, name one element and ask students to suggest a change to make, such as changing the Boy to a Girl. Point out to students that often, when one element changes, the change affects other elements as well. For example, if the setting changes to Lapland, the Boy might be guarding a herd of reindeer instead of sheep.

After each dramatization, you can briefly discuss with students how changing one element affected the story. Be sure that, no matter how your class changes the elements of the story, the moral remains the same.

MAIN ELEMENTS:

CHARACTERS
  the Boy

COULD BECOME:
  a girl, a group of children,
  an old Man/Woman, a security guard

  the Villagers

  a family, school classmates,
  employees of a company

  the Sheep

  cattle, rabbits, precious cargo on a ship

  the Wolf

  coyote, hawks, pirates

SETTING
  village & meadow

COULD BECOME:
  a school, another country, the old West,
  a ship on the sea, a factory, a fairy kingdom

TIME PERIOD
  olden days

COULD BECOME:
  the present, the future, the stone age,
  pioneer days

The Boy Who Cried Wolf
(traditional)

Once there was a boy who lived in a village. His job was to take care of a flock of sheep, so every day he would take the flock to the meadow to eat the fresh grass that grew there. All day long the boy had no one to talk to and nothing to do but watch the sheep, so he was often bored and lonely.

One day, the boy decided to create some excitement. While he was in the meadow with the sheep, he called out, "Wolf! Wolf!" even though there was no wolf in sight. The people in the village heard his cries, dropped whatever work they were doing, and hurried to help rescue the sheep from the wolf. As he watched the villagers frantically run up the mountain, the boy laughed and laughed. The villagers realized that the boy had played a trick on them, so they scolded him and returned to the village.

The boy got such a big kick out of his joke that the next day he did the same thing. Again the villagers came running to help, and again the boy laughed at them and they realized that it was only a trick.

On the third day, the boy was watching his sheep in the meadow when a real wolf suddenly attacked the flock. The boy called to the villagers for help, crying, "Wolf! Wolf!" This time, however, the villagers assumed that he was playing a joke on them again. Not a single person came to rescue the flock and several of the sheep were eaten by the wolf that day.

COMMENTARY:

Fables provide excellent material for dramatizing with young children as they are short and simple, often have animals or natural elements as characters, and have morals that are easy to understand. "The Boy Who Cried Wolf" is particularly excellent for dramatization because the entire class can participate as Villagers. (For more ideas about dramatizing this fable, also see *Creative Drama in the Primary Grades* by Nellie McCaslin.)

VARIATIONS:

Try this lesson with other fables, such as those from Aesop, or with short and well-known fairy tales, such as "The Three Little Pigs" or "Hansel and Gretel." Read variations of familiar tales to your class, for example: "Vasilissa the Beautiful" (a "Cinderella" type story from Russia) or the picture book, *Deep in the Forest* by Brinton Turkle (a variation on "Goldilocks and the Three Bears" in which a little bear comes into the house of some humans).

PART VII
PLAY PRODUCTION

Working with Children in Play Production

More than ten years of working with children to produce plays, music, and dance performances has shown us that performing can be an enriching, enjoyable, and worthwhile experience for young people and for the adults who teach them. The keys to working on amateur performances are: the attitude of the director, adequate planning, and sufficient rehearsal time so that the performers are confident.

When directing plays with children, we recommend you maintain a positive and calm attitude. Always be fully respectful and supportive of every one of your cast members. It's understandable if you, as director, become anxious and demanding in rehearsals due to your desire to have the production meet your standards of excellence and because of your sense of responsibility for its outcome. However, it will be a more productive and enjoyable experience for everyone if you refrain from expressing anxiety and irritation to your students. Keep the production in perspective: Remember, it's not Broadway— it's a group of kids doing their best and hopefully having fun in the process (we've encountered very few children who didn't absolutely love being in plays).

At the same time, expect nothing but the best from your actors. Demand that they pay attention, cooperate with others, and put forth their best efforts. Maintain a rehearsal atmosphere that is disciplined and focused. Be confident in your role as leader and your cast will sense this and react accordingly, respecting your authority and the limits you set. Likewise, if you are unsure of yourself as director your cast will feel insecure, which will then be reflected in their performance.

One of the most difficult aspects of directing children in plays is that they sometimes have a hard time focusing their attention, especially in the beginning. Their excitement about the play may be expressed in boisterous activity, making direction difficult for the adults in charge. Play production teaches children to focus their attention, to work with others, and to take responsibility for their own behavior. Concentrate on teaching your students these skills and remember that they are in the *process* of learning them. Be assured that as rehearsals progress, students will become more able to see how all the parts fit into the big picture of the play and will become more able to concentrate for longer periods of time.

Casting

The following is a suggested method for casting plays with seven- to nine-year-olds. We believe that it's neither appropriate nor necessary to audition students at this age. The method described below accommodates all students' choices as much as possible, and students can see that everyone is treated equally.

1. Read or tell the entire story of the play, using either the script or a picture book of the story. Ask the actors to be thinking about which, if any, characters they would most like to play.

2. Ask the actors to say which roles they most prefer and write their choices on the blackboard where everyone can see them. The actors should name all the roles they are interested in playing, even if others have named the same roles. They can also choose to say if they are willing to play any role, or if they prefer a speaking or nonspeaking role.

3. Review the list together and work to complete the cast list to everyone's satisfaction.
   - Whenever more than one actor wants the same role, you can pull names out of a hat to make the decision. Children appreciate the fairness of this method.

- Some of the characters in this play can be played as either female or male, such as the Dwarves and the Hot'-Hot (Ducks). If you have a limited number of girls or boys, tell students that it's in keeping with theater tradition for females to play male roles and for males to play female roles.
- Roles can be changed from singular to plural or from plural to singular to accommodate your cast. For example, the role of Soup'-kss (Seal) could become a family of seals, or the Children of the Brothers' Sister could become just one child.

Script Preparation

After the cast has been determined, make a photocopy of the script. You can then write in any changes (such as pronoun alterations) on this master copy before making copies for the cast. Each actor need only get a copy of the page(s) in which she or he has speaking lines. With a highlighting pen, mark the actor's lines for each copy and send it home with a note to the child's parents or guardians asking them to help their child memorize her or his lines at home. Students can then keep their script pages at home. Copy the entire script or appendices as needed for other adults who may be helping with your production.

Blocking

Blocking is the planning of all basic stage placement and movement. It is one of the first things you should do in your rehearsal process. Blocking can be tedious, but it's well worth the patience required. Establishing the placement and movement of actors, sets, and props forms a framework for the play and helps to focus the rehearsals. Pay close attention to all blocking of people, props, and sets, and keep accurate notes in your own copy of the script. Each movement affects other parts of the play—a misplaced prop or costume can cause confusion. All the blocking of actors, sets, and props needs to be rehearsed as thoroughly and often as do the speaking lines, so it's best to get started early.

During the blocking process it's often difficult for children to pay attention and remain quiet, especially when they're not in the scene being worked on. In the beginning, they often can't yet understand the big picture and where their character fits in. Over the course of rehearsals all the pieces will come together and the play will jell for them. Until then, don't expect them to pay complete attention when they're not in a scene, and instead set out a quiet activity for them, such as books or drawing materials.

When blocking, use the standard vocabulary for stage directions shown below. Stage directions are from the perspective of the actors when they're facing the audience, i.e., "right" is the actor's right. "Down" refers to the part of the stage closest to the audience and "up" is the part of the stage farthest from the audience.

AUDIENCE

Down Left	Down Center	Down Right
Left	Center	Right
Up Left	Up Center	Up Right

Use many different levels for your stage, such as tabletops or other platforms—a variety of levels makes the staging interesting. If the audience is sitting on the same level as the stage, stage your action as high up as possible, especially if the blocking calls for the actors to be sitting or lying down, otherwise the audience in the back rows will have a hard time seeing.

When planning blocking, be creative with the furniture available to you. Sturdy tables with folding legs can be used as slides by folding up one side of the legs. Slides make for interesting movement and are, needless to say, very popular with kids. Tables, chairs, and other furniture can inspire interesting blocking, as can doors, closets, windows, and other features of the room you use.

Create adequate backstage areas—with enough room for actors, sets, props, and costumes—in places from which the actors can watch the play. If the actors can't see or hear the play, they will swiftly lose interest and focus. It's also more enjoyable for them to be able to watch the show. Make sure you plan the backstage blocking along with the onstage blocking, so that everyone knows exactly where they're supposed to be at all times. If you're working with a large cast, create several backstage areas with a different area assigned to each small group of characters. This will go a long way in maintaining order and quiet.

Use a lot of exciting action that's fun for the kids to perform, and it will be fun for the audience to watch as well. Let them run, jump, skip, fly! Risk a little noise and chaos so that the actors can experience some really exciting movements. Rehearse particularly fast or chaotic action in slow motion first. Always make sure you give clear rules about how to move in the space, and in relation to others, so that everyone is safe.

Repetition in blocking helps children remember what to do (for example, their character always enters from a certain place and exits through a set route). One actor can be assigned to lead group movements, making it easier for the others to follow. Sometimes it's useful for the actors to have an assigned order of movement—who goes first, second, third, and so on—to avoid arguments and to help the actors remember what to do.

Theater Space

The following are a few ideas for being creative with performance space:

- Place the audience around three-quarters of the stage, with your fourth portion being used for backdrops, sets, or backstage.

- Create a theater-in-the-round, where the audience sits in a circle around the stage. The feeling of intimacy can be wonderful and it eliminates the need for large sets or backdrops.

- The entire performance space, including the audience area, can be decorated as the setting of the play, so that the audience is made to feel they are "in" the performance.

- The performance can take place in various locations that the audience must travel to throughout the course of the play, such as the hallway, other rooms or outside.

Rehearsals

Rehearsals with second- and third-graders should generally last between 30–45 minutes, or even up to an hour. Rehearsals can be alternated with production workshops (making the sets, props, or costumes), or with music rehearsals. Always maintain a rehearsal atmosphere that is positive and fun while being focused and under control.

Be open to new ideas generated by students during the first stages of rehearsals. They will most likely come up with great ideas you never thought of, and the actors will feel personally invested in the production if their ideas are heard and, when possible, used. At a certain point, however, you need to establish the artistic decisions so that the play can be rehearsed with consistency and so that everyone can feel secure about what will take place.

After casting and blocking, rehearse individual scenes while creating the production elements (sets, props, and costumes) that are added to rehearsals as they become available. If you don't have all the props available initially, use substitutes so that the actors can get used to them and where they belong. During this time the actors should be memorizing their lines, preferably at home. If they can't remember their lines, encourage the actors to say them in their own words. It's more important that the actors understand what is happening in the story and what their character is intending when they speak than it is for them to say the lines exactly as they are written.

The last few rehearsals should be run-throughs of the entire play. As you get close to the performance day, do a few run-throughs without interruption. Take notes during the run-throughs and go over them with the cast right before the next rehearsal. In addition to your notes, solicit the cast's comments about the run-through and suggestions for future improvements.

For one of your last, dress rehearsals, invite a preview audience. This will go a long way toward helping your actors focus their attention and get past some of their initial nervousness, as well as jelling the play production and working out any problems. At the end of this preview performance, ask the cast to sit on the stage while you solicit the audience's questions and comments. You will be amazed at how much a preview performance will improve your production.

Rehearsal Alternatives

The following are some ideas for fun, alternative rehearsals when you want to make a refreshing change:

- Rehearse the play in fast-forward. Not only is it extremely silly, it's a good way to drill the lines and blocking.

- Run the lines only, while everyone sits or lies down. This is a useful drill and good for when everyone has low energy.

- Do the play in gibberish, so that the actors must express their intent through tone of voice, facial expressions, and gestures. Don't do this if you object to giggling and merriment in your class.

- Switch roles. Seeing what other actors do with their roles can give actors new ideas. It's fine if they substitute their own words for the actual lines.

Basic Acting Skills

At the second- and third-grade level, children should not be expected to be highly skilled actors; however, they are capable of understanding some basic acting skills, including vocal projection and characterization (see Suggestions, below). Movement, another basic acting skill, is included in many of the lessons of this curriculum. You can adapt some of these lessons to augment your play rehearsal process. For example, Lesson 3 has a Move and Freeze activity. Here's one way to adapt those lessons to *Da-Hoos-Wheé-Whee* characters:

1. Call out the name of a character in the play.

2. Give the "Move" signal (such as turning on music or playing a drum beat) and ask students to move around the room as that character would move. You can call out suggestions or questions as they move to encourage them to explore their options. For example: *"How do the Ducks move when they're fighting?"*

3. At the "Freeze" signal, students freeze in a statue of that character. Pause for a few seconds, perhaps making observations about what you see.

4. Call out the name of another character and repeat the process.

Another lesson useful for adapting to rehearsals for *Da-Hoos-Wheé-Whee* would be Lesson 5 (Activity B, "Family Photo Album")

One of the biggest pitfalls of children's play productions is that the actors mumble their lines so that the audience can't hear and understand them. Work with your actors to speak loudly, slowly, and clearly. Help them understand that speaking in a normal, conversational voice will not be effective on the stage. In addition to doing exercises for breathing, diction, and vocal projection, establish your actors' *intention* that the entire audience hear and understand the play. Intention is everything! For example, if you were to see that someone across the street was about to be hit by a car, your intention for them to hear your warning would be very strong and you would automatically have tremendous vocal projection when you said, "Look out!"

Another problem with child actors is that they often merely recite their lines without connecting with the character they are playing. Throughout the rehearsal process, ask your actors about the thoughts, feelings, and intentions of their characters. You can also set up some improvisations of encounters between various characters in the play as well as other scenes that aren't in the script. For example (using characters from *Da-Hoos-Wheé-Whee*): "One day, Da-Hoos-Wheé-Whee were out hunting when they met up with the Tsah'-pah, the old man who had cast the spell on them." Or, "The people of the Lushootseed Village discover that the Brothers' Sister has been lying."

Curtain Call and Post-Play Discussion

After the performance, each actor should be able to take a bow by themselves, perhaps with their name and character announced, to receive their well-deserved applause. Any non-acting stage crew members can also be acknowledged, and in the end, the entire cast and crew can take a bow together. Rehearse the bows and maintain onstage quiet and dignity throughout the curtain call, so that each person gets full attention for their bow.

After the curtain call, the cast can sit on the stage for a post-play discussion with the audience. The director solicits questions and comments from the audience and facilitates the actors' answers. Children love showing off their expertise at this time, and both the curtain call and the post-play discussion build self-esteem.

It's nice to end a performance with a reception, or cast party, with snacks and beverages, when the audience and cast can intermingle. You did it!

Production

The following are some general guidelines for creating all the production elements for a play:

- Be creative with your resources—you don't have to spend a lot of money on materials. Paper, cardboard, markers, duct tape, and large fabric pieces can take care of most of your needs.

- Use the production tasks as activities in creating thinking. While giving the actors practical advice on how to make props or sets, allow them to figure things out and come up with their own ideas for construction and design.

- Prepare each task to be as self-directed as possible. If you thoroughly prepare the materials, the actors can work independently. This will free you from the stress of trying to help several groups make things at the same time, or allow you to rehearse with one group while another group constructs sets or props.

- The directions for making sets, props, costumes, sound, and music listed in the appendices for this script are only suggestions— feel free to use other ideas for creating your own, unique production.

- Sets should be simple and light enough for the children to move by themselves. Large cardboard appliance boxes can be cut to make light, free-standing walls that are good for backdrops. You can tape butcher paper over the wall that students can then paint or color with markers.

- Establish these rules about props with your actors: 1) Props are not toys and should not be played with. 2) Props should only be handled by the actor who uses them and never touched or moved by anyone else. 3) Actors (not the director) should place their own props. Always rehearse with props or prop substitutes.

- A props table can be set up backstage, so that props are not accidentally stepped on or lost.

- Costumes need not be ornate, store-bought, or made by parents. It's possible to simply allow each student to select a colored chiffon scarf or other piece of plain, light fabric. Students can then choose how to wear their scarves as costumes, such as: loosely tied around the neck as a cape, tied around the waist as a belt or skirt, or tied around their forehead as a headband.

- Makeup can be fun but should be optional, for not all children want to wear it and some may be allergic to it. Eye shadow, eyebrow pencil, blusher, and lipstick are easy to obtain and help to emphasize the actors' features. Look for face paints at sale prices right after Halloween.

- Enlist the aid of volunteers to help with your production needs. Many adults enjoy getting involved in play productions, and you will find a wealth of talent and resources among your students' parents. Collaborate with the music and dance/movement specialists at your school to create your show.

Understanding the Dramatic Art:
The Meaning Frame and the Expressive Frame

(Thanks to Norah Morgan and Juliana Saxton, *Teaching Drama*.)

For the classroom teacher to be an effective drama instructor, it is useful to understand some of the basic forms of the art of drama and theater. Drama can be seen as operating in two frames: the *meaning frame*—the inner understanding, oriented toward the participant, and the *expressive frame*—the outer manifestation, oriented toward the audience. In our first chapter, "Why Drama in the Classroom?" we described the spectrum of drama activities for the classroom, from creative dramatics to theater. Creative dramatics, or process-oriented activities with improvised dialogue and action (including role drama) is primarily concerned with the meaning frame. Theater involves the use of elements and techniques for the purpose of communicating to an audience and can be seen as being primarily concerned with the expressive frame. Play production for public performance is an example of the expressive frame.

Morgan and Saxton have this to say about the relationship between creative dramatics and theater: "Drama and theatre are not mutually exclusive. If drama is about meaning, it is the art form of theatre which encompasses and contains that meaning. If theatre is about expression, then it is the dramatic exploration of the meaning which fuels that expression."

The Elements of Theater

The elements described below are typically associated with theater craft, and a general knowledge of these basic elements is pertinent to a classroom play production. In addition, an understanding of these elements can be applied to other classroom drama activities as well, including creative dramatics, role drama, and story dramatizations. Classroom teachers can make full use of these elements to spark interest, to maintain concentration and motivation, and to crystallize the shared experience of the drama activity. The essential elements of theater craft are: *focus, tension or conflict, contrast,* and *symbol*.

In theater, one must *focus* on the big picture—the overall theme or meaning of the play or other work—as well as focus on the parts that make up the whole: the scenes and other details and how they contribute to an understanding of overall theme. Teachers must also focus on both the educational objectives for each lesson and the dramatic focus of the lesson that will further the realization of those objectives.

Tension, also referred to as *conflict,* is the excitement generated in a drama activity or a play that stimulates interest and motivates participants (or, in a play, the characters) to proceed with the unfolding of events. In classroom drama activities, tension is created by challenges, limits on time or space, fear of the unknown, and other factors. Teachers can inject tension into a drama activity by introducing some type of constraint: "We must escape before the guards wake up!" or challenge: "No one has ever returned from that planet—are you still willing to go?" In a play, the *conflict* is the problem around which the plot revolves (see The Traditional Stages of a Play, below) and which creates the tension at the core of the story.

Interest in drama can also be stimulated by using *contrast* (also known as "the spectra of theater"). These are the elements that create interest, focus, or tension by virtue of contrast. The contrast of light or darkness can be employed, obviously, by adjusting the lights and window blinds in the room. Equally effective is requiring students to close their eyes and asking them to imagine darkness in the room and to continue to imagine it even after they open their eyes. The contrast of sound/silence can be created with a sound signal (see Sound Story in Lesson 4) or by the teacher in role saying something like, "Quiet! I think I hear the spaceships coming!" Movement/stillness can be evoked by a "Freeze/Unfreeze" signal (see Move and Freeze activity in Lesson 3) or by the teacher in role: "If we move even a tiny bit the snakes may attack!" Yet another contrast is called *peripeteia*—the expected/unexpected. Some examples of this contrast include: a powerful warlord who turns out to be a gentle coward, or finding helium balloons at the bottom of the ocean.

Symbol refers to the act of assigning meaning to something, such as a word, an object, or an image. Symbols can have meaning for the collective experience, such as, "This 'talking stick' represents the right to speak in our community." A symbol can also be endowed with meaning by individuals; for example, a "talking stick" might represent the wisdom of the elders for one person; and for another, it represents the power of voice. Symbolization is central to culture and civilization—all artistic endeavors are acts of symbolization.

The Traditional Stages of a Play

As in literature, the essential elements of a play are: *characters, setting* (location and time period), *plot* (the story), and *symbol* (see above). In Western culture, plays have traditionally followed a form of four basic stages: *exposition, rising action, climax,* and *resolution.* This is not to say that this is the only acceptable form for plays and other types of literature but rather that it has historically proven to be an effective means of telling stories and engaging interest in them. Teachers should be aware of these stages in planning, executing, and assessing drama activities. These stages apply to the role drama, "The Mystery Letter," as well as to the lessons that are more typically associated with theater craft, such as Parts VI and VII in this curriculum ("Drama and Literature," and "Play Production").

Exposition, also called *introduction,* is the part of a play that introduces the primary characters, the setting, and the situation. The exposition establishes the conflict or problem that is central to the plot and that motivates the characters to action. In this book, Chapter 6, "Starting Out: Creating a Context," is akin to the exposition of a play for it introduces the context of this drama curriculum and the role drama, "The Mystery Letter."

Rising action, also known as *complications* or *complicating action,* refers to the actions and events that arise out of the central conflict or problem of the play and that lead to the climax. In this book, the rising action begins with the e-mail message to the Designers from the Postmaster General, inviting them to enter the postage stamp design competition. The rising action continues through the Designers' research on Postal Workers and their investigation of the Mystery Letter in Parts 2 and 3.

Climax, also called *crisis,* is the high point of a play, where the central conflict or problem of the play reaches its most dramatic and final turning point. In this book, the role drama reaches its climax in "The Mystery Letter, Part 3—The Designers Search for the Recipient of the Letter" and "The Mystery Letter, Part 4—Rendezvous at the Post Office."

Resolution, also referred to as *conclusion* or *dénouement,* is the final section of a play, when the conflict or problem is resolved. By this time, the primary characters will have learned something as a result of the conflict/resolution of the story, and, ideally, the audience will have gained some new understanding as well. In this book, the role drama reaches its conclusion in "The Mystery Letter, Part 4—Rendezvous at the Post Office" and with the awarding of the postage stamp design contract to the Designers at the Public Sharing Event.

Da-Hoos-Wheé-Whee
"The Seal Hunting Brothers,"
traditional Lushootseed Salish
Script by Pamela Gerke from the retelling by Vi Hilbert

This story comes from the Lushootseed Salish, the Native American or "First People" of the Puget Sound region of Western Washington, near Seattle. The Lushootseed have a rich oral tradition that has only been translated into written form in the last few decades. This script is adapted from *Haboo, Native American Stories of Puget Sound* by Vi Hilbert, translator and editor of much of Lushootseed oral tradition, as told by Martha LaMont at Tulalip, Washington, in 1966. Her exact wording has been preserved, except for a few slight changes for the sake of clarity or brevity. Vi Hilbert has given her blessing for this adaptation of the story into play format for children.

There are many tribes in the Puget Sound region, each with their own language and traditions. The Lushootseed Salish words and story in this play are specifically from the area north of the present Snohomish-King County line, just north of Seattle. We've included a short write-up about Lushootseed Salish culture in Appendix F, as information on Lushootseed Salish culture may otherwise prove difficult or impossible to find.

This story tells of the epic journey of two intrepid brothers who are bewitched by the evil grandfather of their sister's husband. The brothers go on a "spirit journey" into the unknown and come back home empowered by their experience, singing their "spirit songs." A "spirit journey" is when a person goes on a journey of self-discovery and comes back with the wisdom of self-knowledge or spiritual insight. Spirit journeys are respected in the culture of the First People and many are recorded as stories.

"Spirit songs" are personal songs that are given to each person by spiritual powers. The singing of a person's own spirit songs brings them strength and energy. The songs included in Appendix E reportedly have an origin in Native American songs, but they have been altered and adapted over many years and many campfires and in no way presume to emulate Lushootseed musical tradition.

We've selected this play to include in this drama curriculum for second and third grade because it shows both family members and members of communities living together and responding to each other in various ways—some with generosity, others with deception, some with bravery, others with self-interest, and some with love.

Running time of show: (approximate) 25–30 minutes

Rehearsal time needed: 12–15 hours

Other production time needed: 4–6 hours

Cast size:
> **Minimum:** 10, plus Narrator (Except for Da-Hoos-Wheé-Whee, all other actors can play more than one role. The Dwarf lines can be consolidated.)
> **Maximum:** 30

Gender of characters: Soup'kss, Dwarves, Hot'-hot, Chuh-hoo-loo' and Villagers can be played as either female or male; all other characters should be played as designated.

Production needs: see Appendixes B–E

CHARACTERS:
> NARRATOR—(Can be read by an adult or older student)
> DA-HOOS-WHEÉ-WHEE—the Seal Hunting Brothers
> OLDER BROTHER
> YOUNGER BROTHER
> SISTER—of the Brothers
> MAN—husband of their Sister
> CHILDREN—of Sister and Man
> TSAH'-PAH—grandfather of Man
> MAN'S BROTHERS
> SOUP'-KSS—seal
> DWARVES
> OLD MAN DWARF

HOT'-HOT—ducks
HOT'-HOT SIAB—Head Man of the ducks
KAI'-YAH—grandmother of Seal-Hunting Brothers
CHUH-HOO-LOO'—whale
LITTLE BROTHER—of Seal-Hunting Brothers
STEPMOTHER—of Little Brother
BAHD—father of Seal-Hunting Brothers and Little Brother
YOUNG WOMAN
SPIRIT POWERS
GAME: (Optional) DEER, SMELT, BEAR, OTHER

SCENE 1

Note: See "Blocking" in the introductory section to this play for descriptions of stage directions. See Appendices for more information about sets, props, costumes, music, and sound as well as about Lushootseed language, culture, and history

Setting: A Lushootseed village on Puget Sound, long ago. There are 2-3 large, sturdy tables upstage that will be longhouses for both the Lushootseed village and the village of the DWARVES. The facade of each house may either be made by hanging cloth from the tabletops to the floor, downstage, or by setting free-standing cardboard walls in front of the tables. Behind the tables, upstage, are chairs or other means of access to the table-tops for the HOT'-HOT in Scene 3. There is a fire pit set in front of the center longhouse.

There is space downstage for the beach and the ocean—some of the ocean scenes could also take place in the aisles of the audience. The canoes can be made either with a small, children's wagon or out of cardboard boxes with the bottoms cut out, propelled by the actors as they walk inside a box while holding up the sides with their hands. LIGHTS UP.

NARRATOR: This is a story from the Lushootseed Salish of Western Washington. The story begins in a village by the saltwater of Puget Sound. These were the people who lived there: a man, his wife, and his *Tsah'-pah*, his grandfather...

(MAN, SISTER, & TSAH'-PAH enter one at a time as their names are called. MAN exits to one side while SISTER & TSAH'-PAH go into house, center.)

NARRATOR: ...and also her two young brothers, who were seal-hunting brothers, *Da-hoos-wheé-whee.*

(DA-HOOS-WHEÉ-WHEE enter in canoe, and during the following narration they get out of canoe and carry fish to their SISTER'S house.)

NARRATOR: These brothers were great hunters on land and on the water. When they hunted out on the saltwater, they used their *tkl'-ai*, their canoe, which they themselves had made.

(SISTER comes out of house and DA-HOOS-WHEÉ-WHEE give her the fish. She takes it and goes back inside and they exit.)

NARRATOR: The brother-in-law of the hunters arrived.

(MAN enters as SISTER comes out of her house.)

MAN: *Tsi siab!* Hello!

SISTER: *Siab!*

MAN: Did your brothers give you any of the game that they got?

SISTER: *Whee!* No! They don't give us anything.

(MAN, angry, exits. During the following narration, DA-HOOS-WHEÉ-WHEE enter, give SISTER more food, which she takes inside her house, then exit.)

NARRATION: She has, however, been given food. Her brothers give her *soup'-kss*, seal, and porpoise and fish that they have already cooked for her. They expect her to set some aside for her husband to eat when he returns from his work.

(MAN enters as SISTER comes out of her house.)

MAN: *Tsi siab!*

SISTER: *Siab!*

MAN: Did your brothers give you any of the game that they get?

SISTER: *Whee!* They don't give us anything.

(MAN, angry, exits. CHILDREN come out of their house with platters of food and greedily gobble it all—pantomime.)

NARRATOR: Each time her brothers bring food for their sister and her family, she and her children eat all of it. She never sets aside anything for her husband. She has her children sprinkle ashes from the fire on their wooden platters.

(They do so—pantomime.)

NARRATOR: She rubs their mouths with the ashes to hide any traces of grease from the food that they have eaten.

(She does so—pantomime.)

SISTER: Be very quiet and pretend to be hungry!

(MAN enters.)

MAN: *Tsi siab!*

SISTER: *Siab!*

MAN: Your brothers, as usual, have not given you any food?

SISTER: *Whee!* They don't give us anything. Just look at your children, they have had nothing to eat!

(CHILDREN whimper.)

SISTER: The same is true for myself!

NARRATOR: Now the man became very angry and he talked to his brothers and his *Tsah'-pah*, his grandfather.

(SISTER & CHILDREN go into house while MAN'S BROTHERS & TSAH'-PAH enter.)

MAN: What do you think about our killing our brothers-in-law, *Da-hoos-wheé-whee?*

BROTHER #1: Just restrain yourself.

TSAH'-PAH: We shall just put a spell on them! You will pretend to see something way over on the other side of the harbor, and you will come and say to them, "There is a big *soup'-kss*, a seal way over there. You could sneak up on it, you are such good hunters!"

MAN & BROTHERS: *Aiii!* Yes!

(MAN'S BROTHERS & TSAH'-PAH exit while DA-HOOS-WHEÉ-WHEE enter and MAN goes up to them.)

NARRATOR: The woman's husband went to his brothers-in-law and spoke to them as the old man had told him to.

DA-HOOS-WHEÉ-WHEE: *Aiii!* You don't have to say anymore, we're going! *Huy!*

(MAN exits as DA-HOOS-WHEÉ-WHEE get into canoe and paddle out to sea while SOUP'-KSS enters, splashing in water and making seal noises.)

NARRATOR: They could see that there was indeed a great *soup'-kss* out on the water, bending backwards and making noises as seals usually do. However, it was the work of the bad old man. He made the *soup'-kss* and instructed it to take *Da-hoos-wheé-whee* far across the ocean to the very edge. The young men went and harpooned the *soup'-kss*.

(DRUMS & RATTLES BEGIN—fast and frenzied. OLDER BROTHER, while holding the end of the harpoon rope, throws the harpoon. SOUP'-KSS catches it and holds it, as if speared. SOUP'-KSS thrashes about wildly while DA-HOOS-WHEÉ-WHEE are tossed around in their canoe. OLDER BROTHER continues to hold the end of the rope—his hand is magically stuck fast to it. DRUMS & RATTLES lower in volume and continue under the following.)

OLDER BROTHER: Maybe we have had a spell put on us by our brother-in-law's *Tsah'-pah!*

YOUNGER BROTHER: We'll let this *soup'-kss* take us wherever it will!

(DRUMS come up in volume and continue as LIGHTS DOWN. Cedar log is brought onstage and SOUP'-KSS actor attaches harpoon rope to it and exits. DA-HOOS-WHEÉ-WHEE remain onstage. The set remains as is for now while the following scene is played in another area of the stage.)

SCENE 2

Setting: the shore near the village of the DWARVES, the next morning. DRUMS END. LIGHTS UP.

NARRATOR: It was night when the *soup'-kss* arrived with them at a certain place. There was land nearby. They had been released! There floating in front of them was a great big log of cedar, *huh-pai'*, covered with tangled roots and branches. The Older Brother began pulling at his harpoon line, and it took him right to the big, branchy, floating *huh-pai'* log.

(He does so.)

OLDER BROTHER: That evil old man put a spell on us, and that is why we are far away!

YOUNGER BROTHER: It seems we have been taken clear across the ocean. We had better lift up our *tkl'-ai* and hide it.

OLDER BROTHER: *Aiii!*

(They beach their canoe and hide behind it.)

NARRATOR: There they were hiding when they saw a child come into view in a large *tkl'-ai*.

(DWARF #1 enters in a canoe. He acts out the following.)

NARRATOR: Suddenly he began to go to and fro from one end of the *tkl'-ai* to the other. Then he got down and he dove. He was there at the bottom of the ocean for some time. Suddenly he surfaced and he was holding several halibut.

(DWARF #1 puts halibut in his canoe. He acts out the following.)

NARRATOR: Again the child dove. The brothers' mouths were watering as they saw the good food that this creature was getting. They decided to help themselves to his halibut before he came up from his dive.

(DA-HOOS-WHEÉ-WHEE sneak over to DWARF #1's canoe, take the fish, return to their hiding place and hungrily eat the fish. DWARF #1 emerges from the water and gets into his canoe.)

NARRATOR: When the child discovered his fish were missing, this is what he did—*he pointed toward the shore to where they were!* They still think it is a child. However, this person is what people call a dwarf, an old one.

DWARF #1: *(thinking aloud)* I had better take these strange people who come from somewhere. And I shall also take their *tkl'-ai*.

(DWARF #1 goes to shore, grabs DA-HOOS-WHEÉ-WHEE and puts them in his canoe then gets in and begins to paddle.)

DWARF #1: *(to the Brothers)* Don't be afraid. One of our children will come for you.

NARRATOR: Now the two brothers knew that Dwarves had kidnapped them. They are grown adults yet they are small like children.

(ALL exit. LIGHTS DOWN. MUSIC UP while set is changed.)

SCENE 3

Setting: The village of the DWARVES, a few minutes later. The facades of the longhouses are very colorful and fanciful. Either hang colorful cloths from the tabletops or turn around the free-standing walls to show a colorful side. There is a fire pit in front of the center house—same as for scene 1—and a huge pile of dentalium shells near the shore, downstage. DWARVES enter and position themselves about the village. A few HOT'-HOT perch on the longhouse roofs. LIGHTS UP. MUSIC ENDS.

NARRATOR: The people who lived there were not the usual kind of people. There were lots of Dwarves walking around all over— little tiny people, yet they are grown-ups. The dentalia were piled high. This was their food. It was a shellfish that they could get when the tide was out. These shells were things that *Da-hoos-wheé-whee* prized.

(DWARF #1 & DA-HOOS-WHEÉ-WHEE enter in the canoe, go to the village and beach the canoe there. DA-HOOS-WHEÉ-WHEE gape at the pile of shells. DWARF #1 leads them to the longhouses and they sit in front of the fire pit. Other DWARVES gather around and stare at them.)

OLD MAN: *(to Dwarves)* Look at these people. They are really people, wherever it is that they come from. Get busy and prepare some food. It should just be some soup, because they're very weak now and their stomachs aren't very strong.

(Some DWARVES bring out bowls and give them to DA-HOOS-WHEÉ-WHEE who eat out of them—pantomime.)

OLD MAN: This is the land of the Dwarves where you have come.

DWARF #2: We can communicate with those salmon and *hot'-hot,* ducks of all kinds. Our language is the same!

NARRATOR: The brothers looked longingly at the *hot'-hot.* They enjoyed eating duck. Meanwhile, *Kaí-yah,* their grandmother, mourned for the lost brothers.

(ALL freeze. LIGHTS DOWN. LIGHTS UP on KAÍ-YAH who stands off to one side, perhaps on a table.)

NARRATOR: She mourned the loss of *Da-hoos-wheé-whee*. She could see a *soup'-kss* emerge as she cried out her sorrow in the song she sang there by the water's edge.

(MUSIC BEGINS. KAÍ-YAH sings while SOUP'-KSS swims in front of her. There may be a drum accompaniment. See Appendix E for the music.)

KAÍ-YAH: *(singing)*
That is the game that you hunt
Emerging from the water, my child.
(Sing 4 times.)

(MUSIC ENDS, LIGHTS DOWN on KAÍ-YAH. She and SOUP'-KSS exit. LIGHTS UP on village of the DWARVES. ALL un-freeze.)

NARRATOR: Now the Dwarves and the *Hot'-hot* raided and fought each other.

(Note: Rehearse the following battle scene in slow motion until students are able to safely control their actions and voices.)

(DRUMS & RATTLES BEGIN: fast and furious. The HOT'-HOT on the rooftops jump off and more HOT'-HOT enter and all chase the DWARVES with loud duck cries. The HOT'-HOT stab their feathers at the DWARVES and when a DWARF gets hit, the actor holds the feather against her or his body as if pierced by the arrow and dies. At first, DA-HOOS-WHEÉ-WHEE hide and watch the battle, then they take the canoe paddles and chase the HOT'-HOT, hitting and killing some. DRUMS & RATTLES lower in volume under the following:)

HOT'-HOT SIAB: Raise your arms, my brothers! Those are human beings who are doing you in! Raise your arms, my brothers! Those are human beings who are doing you in!

(DRUMS raise in volume as HOT'-HOT flap their wings, squawking loudly, and fly away in fright. DRUMS END. DA-HOOS-WHEÉ-WHEE look around at the dead Dwarves. One of them pulls a feather out of DWARF #3 and she or he instantly comes back to life.)

DWARF #3: I'm alive! I'm alive!

(DA-HOOS-WHEÉ-WHEE continue to pull all the feathers out of the DWARVES and they all come back to life.)

ALL DWARVES: *(when each is restored)* I'm alive! I'm alive!

NARRATOR: The brothers took the dead *Hot'-hot* off to one side. They cooked them and feasted a little.

(They do so. Meanwhile, DWARVES gather together.)

DWARF #4: These human beings have done us such a good deed, how can we return them to their home?

DWARF #5: They have given us life! Those *Hot'-hot* have been killing us for a long time.

DWARF #6: What can we do to get them back to their own homeland?

NARRATOR: The brothers were told that they would be taken home. The brothers went to the discarded dentalium shells and sorted out the biggest ones they could find.

(DA-HOOS-WHEÉ-WHEE get some woven bags and fill them with shells. Meanwhile, the DWARVES gather around them.)

DWARF #7: We are going to return you folks. We shall call the *chuh-hoo-loó*, the whale who travels all around. He will return you to your home.

DWARF #8: That *chuh-hoo-loó* is an old person!

(DWARVES go to shore and call out.)

DWARVES: *Chuh-hoo-loó! Chuh-hoo-loó!* (and so forth)

(CHUH-HOO-LOÓ enters.)

DWARF #9: *(to Chuh-hoo-loó)* We want you to return the two brothers, along with their *tkl'-ai*.

DWARF #10: Take them way over there. You know where they are from.

CHUH-HOO-LOÓ: *Aiii,* I know where these people are from. I pass by their homeland and I can hear an old woman mourning out loud. She must be their *kaí-yah.*

(DA-HOOS-WHEÉ-WHEE climb onto the whale's back with their bags of shells.)

CHUH-HOO-LOÓ: I forbid a young female to look at me. If it is her moon-time, that is a serious taboo. The minute her eyes were to see me I would go into convulsions and thrash about!

(Note: "Moon-time" refers to menstruation. Students can also be told that this refers to "when the moon is full.")

(They swim out to sea and exit. LIGHTS DOWN and MUSIC UP during set change.)

SCENE 4

Setting: the Lushootseed village, a few weeks later. LIGHTS UP. CHUH-HOO-LOÓ & DA-HOOS-WHEÉ-WHEE enter.

NARRATOR: They traveled along until they could see a place where there were people living. Suddenly a young woman peeked at him.

(YOUNG WOMAN enters and looks at CHUH-HOO-LOÓ. DRUMS BEGIN: fast and wild. CHUH-HOO-LOÓ goes into convulsions, causing DA-HOOS-WHEÉ-WHEE to be tossed about. Their shells get scattered into the water and they fall in as well. They swim ashore while CHUH-HOO-LOÓ exits. Meanwhile, YOUNG WOMAN has exited. DRUMS END.)

NARRATOR: They felt sad about their dentalia spilling out. Their spirit powers came to them as they felt sad about all the misfortune they had had to endure.

(SPIRIT POWERS enter and stand near DA-HOOS-WHEÉ-WHEE.)

NARRATOR: They were seen by a child who was out playing.

(LITTLE BROTHER enters.)

LITTLE BROTHER: *Siab!*

DA-HOOS-WHEÉ-WHEE: *Siab!* Are you our little brother?

LITTLE BROTHER: *Aiii!* We have been watching for you for a long time. Our people have suffered a lot of hardship and misery since you were lost.

OLDER BROTHER: You go home and tell the people that they are to gather everyone together. We will enter their home then. As soon as we come in we will sing our spirit songs.

LITTLE BROTHER: *Aiii!*

(LITTLE BROTHER goes over to village as VILLAGERS & STEPMOTHER enter there.)

LITTLE BROTHER: My brothers are over there. They told me to come and tell you to gather everyone together, then they will come here and come inside.

STEPMOTHER: You dirty little thing, do you have to say something like that to us!

(She strikes him. He runs back to DA-HOOS-WHEÉ-WHEE.)

(Note: The Stepmother should slap her own hand, holding it close to Little Brother, without actually striking him.)

LITTLE BROTHER: My people just beat me! They think that I am only talking.

YOUNGER BROTHER: You go ahead and tell them that we are their children who have come. We will go there and go inside only after they have followed our instructions, because we want to sing our spirit songs now.

(LITTLE BROTHER goes back to village and pantomimes talking with BAHD.)

NARRATOR: The bad woman who beat him is just his stepmother. However, his father, *Bahd,* begins to believe his little son. He has everyone put things in order to welcome those who have been lost.

(ALL VILLAGERS enter and gather around village. DA-HOOS-WHEÉ-WHEE & SPIRIT POWERS come over to them during the following narration.)

NARRATOR: The brothers then come. Just as soon as they enter they begin to sing their spirit songs.

(MUSIC BEGINS. See Appendix E for music.)

DA-HOOS-WHEÉ-WHEE & SPIRIT POWERS: *(singing)*
We all fly like eagles
Flying so high
Circle 'round the universe
With wings of pure light
Hoo-wit-chee-chi-o
Hoo-we-i-o
Hoo-wit-chee-chi-o
Hoo-we-i-o

(MUSIC ENDS.)

NARRATOR: Now things were changed. Deer and other food came down toward the shore.

(Optional—DEER enters.)

NARRATOR: Smelt came out of the water. All of the food came freely of its own accord. The bear came, and the *sou´p-kss*, along with other food.

(Optional—SMELT, BEAR, SOU´P-KSS, and OTHER GAME enter.)

NARRATOR: That was what happened, and they all sang their spirit songs until everyone's power was strengthened.

(MUSIC BEGINS: drums, rattles, and so on See Appendix E for music.)

ALL: *(singing)*
    The earth is our mother
    We must take care of her
    The earth is our mother
    We must take care of her
    Hey-yung-a, ho-yung-a
    Hey-yung-yung
    Hey-yung-a, ho-yung-a
    Hey-yung-yung.

    Her sacred ground we walk upon
    With every step we take
    Her sacred ground we walk upon
    With every step we take
    Hey-yung-a, ho-yung-a
    Hey-yung-yung
    Hey-yung-a, ho-yung-a
    Hey-yung-yung.

(MUSIC ENDS.)

NARRATOR: That is the end of the story concerning those who were lost.

ALL: *Hoi'-yah!* All is finished!

(LIGHTS DOWN.)

THE END

APPENDIX A
VOCABULARY LIST
OF FOREIGN LANGUAGE

Lushootseed
English
Pronunciation

aiii
> *yes*
> a'-eee

bahd
> *father*
> baad

chuh-hoo-loó
> *whale*
> chuh-hoo-loo' (blow breath out, fast, on middle syllable)

da-hoos-wheé-whee
> *seal-hunting brothers, "the ones who hunt"*
> dah-hoos-wheé-whee (blow breath out on second, third, and
> fourth syllables)

hoi'-yah
> *the end*
> hoy'-awh

hot'-hot
> *ducks*
> hot'-hot

huh-pai'
> *cedar*
> huh-pie'ee

huy
> *good-bye*
> hoi

kaí-yah
> *grandmother*
> ki'-yah

siab
> *head man, or chief*
> see'-ahb

soup'-kss
> *seal*
> soup'-kss (catch in throat on "k")

tkl'-ai
> *canoe*
> kl-eye (make clicking sound in back of throat on "k")

tsah'-pah
> *grandfather*
> tsah'-pah

tsi siab / siab
> *hello (said to females / males)*
> tsee' see-ab / see'-ab

whee
> *no*
> whee (blow breath and pull in quickly at the end)

APPENDIX B
SETS

LUSHOOTSEED VILLAGE
Use 2–3 large, sturdy tables and do one of the following: Tape plain, dark cloths to hang from tabletops to the floor, downstage, or make 2–3 freestanding walls out of cardboard, decorate as longhouse facades using paint or markers, and place in front of the tables, downstage.

DWARF VILLAGE
Use the same tables as for the Lushootseed village (or set up 2–3 other tables on the opposite side of the stage). Do one of the following: Hang colorful cloths from the tabletops to the floor, downstage, or make 2–3 freestanding walls out of cardboard (or use the reverse side of the walls used for the Lushootseed village), decorate very colorfully as longhouse facades using paint or markers, and place in front of the tables, downstage.

FIRE PIT
Use several cardboard paper towel tubes or other cardboard pieces, rolled liked logs. Tape them onto a flat piece of cardboard. Take red, orange, or yellow tissue paper, rip into large pieces, place the pieces under and around the logs, and tape them down with clear tape so that they jut up and out like flames.

CEDAR LOG
Use a large piece of sturdy cardboard, roll it into a tube and secure the shape with strong tape. Paint it brown. Branches and leaves can be made out of cardboard and colored paper (or use real branches).

Make a few small cuts in the log, jab the ends of the branches into the holes and secure them from inside the trunk with strong tape.

LARGE PILE OF DENTALIUM SHELLS

Roll a large piece of cardboard to make a cone or mound shape and tape to secure the shape. Paint the cone or mound white. To make the shells: Cut white paper into squares approximately 10 cm square; place a pencil on the corner of each square and tightly roll the paper around the pencil at a diagonal. (These shells are larger than most real dentalium shells but as props they should be large.) With a single dab of glue on each shell, affix them to the cone or mound. You can also draw more shells on the cone or mound with a marker. Also make extra shells for placing loosely around the bottom on the pile, for the brothers to pick up and put in their bags.

LANDSCAPE BACKDROP (OPTIONAL)

Cut a large piece of butcher paper to fit across upstage wall. With markers or paint, draw scenes of the shores of Puget Sound. Make sure the artists understand which end is up, and that drawings must be large enough to be seen from the audience. Tape to the wall.

APPENDIX C
PROPS

CANOES (2)

You can either use children's wagons or large cardboard boxes. To use wagons: Actors sit in the wagons with the handles turned inward and propel the wagons with one foot on the floor, upstage. Cover the sides of the wagon with cardboard or butcher paper and paint to decorate as a canoe. To use boxes: Cut or fold and tape both the tops and the bottoms. Paint the outside of the boxes. Actors propel the boat by walking inside the boxes while holding up the sides with their hands.

PADDLES (2)
Use thick, sturdy cardboard and cut into the shape of two paddles. Reinforce them by laying a dowel or other wooden stick down the length each of the paddles and securing with tape. Paint brown.

HARPOON
On thick, sturdy cardboard, draw and cut out a spear point with a wide rectangle at its base. Lay the spear point cutout on top of the end of a dowel or other wooden stick. Wrap strong tape around the base of the spear point (the rectangle) to secure it to the stick. Cut a length of rope several meters long. Tie one end of the rope to the unpointed end of the stick and tape it down for extra security.

DUCK FEATHERS (SEVERAL)
Use real feathers and plastic straws. Jab the end of each feather into the end of a plastic straw. If needed, tape the feathers to the straws to secure.

FISH
Use plastic fish or cut fish out of construction paper and decorate with markers.

WOODEN PLATTERS
2 WOODEN SOUP BOWLS
2 NET BAGS

APPENDIX D
COSTUMES

DA-HOOS-WHEÉ-WHEE & ALL VILLAGERS: traditional Lushootseed costumes, or plain pants and shirts

SOUP'-KSS: plain gray or black leotard and tights or pants and shirt

DWARVES: colorful pants and shirts

DUCKS: plain colored pants and shirts with plastic duckbills or duckbill baseball-type hats and wings made of cloth pinned to shirt sleeves

CHUH-HOO-LOÓ: plain gray or black leotard and tights or pants and shirt

SPIRIT POWERS: fanciful costumes, perhaps with gauze fabric capes and headpieces

BEAR, DEER, SMELT, & OTHER GAME: plain colored pants and shirts or leotard and tights, with ears, tails, and so forth added

APPENDIX E
SOUND AND MUSIC

When Da-hoos-wheé-whee chase phantom soup'-kss: drums and rattles

During Dwarves & Hot'-hot battle: drums and rattles

"The Earth Is Our Mother"—song included

"Kaí-yah's Song"—song included

"We All Fly Like Eagles"—song included

THE EARTH IS OUR MOTHER

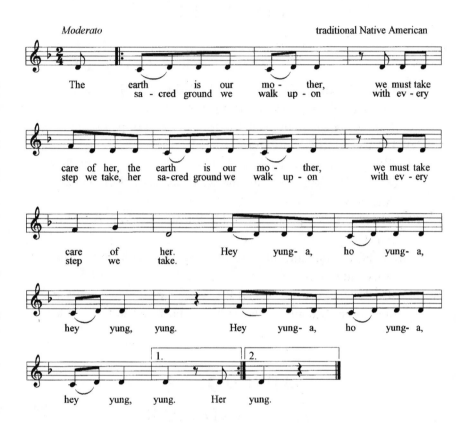

Moderato traditional Native American

The earth is our mo - ther, we must take
sa - cred ground we walk up - on with ev - ery

care of her, the earth is our mo - ther, we must take
step we take, her sa - cred ground we walk up - on with ev - ery

care of her. Hey yung- a, ho yung- a,
step we take.

hey yung, yung. Hey yung- a, ho yung- a,

1. hey yung, yung. **2.** Her yung.

KAI-YAH'S SONG

tune: Pamela Gerke

Moderately

That is the game that you hunt E - merg ing from the

wa - ter my child.

WE ALL FLY LIKE EAGLES

APPENDIX F
LUSHOOTSEED SALISH CULTURE

LITERATURE

In the past, all elements of the culture of these peoples had to be committed to memory; thus, their historians developed excellent memories in order to pass on important information to later generations. When the culture was solely oral, as some elders would prefer to have it remain, the legends were recited often in order to keep them alive and point out moral lessons. We do not know how long it has taken for these stories to come down to us, for the Salish did not use the kind of calendar we use today. The Lushootseed peoples marked time by referring to especially remarkable occasions, such as the year of the solar eclipse or the time before the British people came. Today, the art of storytelling among the Lushootseed-speaking peoples is nearly forgotten as television and books have supplanted the roles of the Lushootseed raconteurs.

All of the Lushootseed Salish legends are like gems with many facets. They need to be read, savored, and reread from many angles. Listeners are expected to listen carefully and discover why a story is being told. Listeners are not told the meaning of the stories directly but are instead allowed the dignity of finding their own personal interpretation. All of the stories in Lushootseed culture are rich in humor, much of which pokes fun at pretentiousness. The Lushootseed can laugh at themselves and others in a way that is not malicious and that is mutually enjoyable and frequently uplifting.

LANGUAGE

Lushootseed is one of some twenty Native languages comprising the Salish family, spoken throughout much of Washington, British Columbia, and parts of Idaho, Montana, and Oregon. Lushootseed itself is the name of the Native language of the Puget Sound region, of which there are many dialects.

Translating the literature of one language into another is never easy, especially when the cultures involved are extremely dissimilar and when the translator must render in writing what has been an oral tradition. Subtleties of the Lushootseed language and oral delivery, such as tone of voice, vocal mannerisms, rhythm, pitch, and the effects of syntax and repetitions, cannot be fully expressed in written English. For example, there is no Lushootseed word for love, so its meaning and nuances must be recognized through the signals expressed in the oral delivery.

In Lushootseed culture, everything is possible because they have no word for *can't*. They also have no words that say "hello," "good morning," "good night," or "thank you." All these meanings are expressed through phrases or by physical gestures. For example, thankfulness is expressed by using a saying that translates as "You have done me a great favor / I appreciate what you have done for me" or by raising both arms and slightly moving the open palms up and down.

SPIRITUAL VALUES

All of the Lushootseed stories give expression to the most important values of the culture. These values, as remembered and translated by Vi Hilbert, are listed below. Many of the Lushootseed values are phrased in the negative but are here expressed in the positive:

Respect (Hold Sacred) all of the Earth
Respect (Hold Sacred) All of the Spirits
Remember (Hold Sacred) the Creator
Be Honest (Don't You Dare Lie!)
Be Generous (Be Helpful to Your People In Any Way You Can!)
Be Compassionate (Feel Forgiveness For Others!)
Be Clean (You Will Be Washed / Keep Washing Away All Badness
  [Dirt and Sin-Crime])
Be Industrious (And You Will Work Always, Don't Be Lazy!)

Today, many Lushootseed people are preserving and activating the spiritual beliefs of their ancestors. In the past, Lushootseed people believed they needed a spirit power to help them with special tasks. At around age four, boys went away by themselves to fast and wait for their spirit powers to make themselves known. Women also had spirit helpers for their special tasks. Animals, fish, and everything in nature each possessed a spirit, just as humans do. Ceremonies were created to show good intentions to the spirits. For example, the bones of the salmon were thrown back into the water in order to thank the salmon spirits, and so that new salmon would be generated from them.

SOCIAL VALUES

Lushootseed peoples are told again and again to not disgrace themselves or their people under any circumstances. Still, they appreciate anyone smart enough to get something done by fooling someone else. Their stories are often about people with animal names so that the humor of human foibles and frailties can be more openly laughed about.

In public, however, Native people take care to not make anyone feel embarrassed or unwanted, and they genuinely appreciate differences between people. Although the characters in their stories often get themselves in lots of trouble, they are not wiped out in the end. Instead, they are allowed to stew in their own folly, and figure their own way out of the situation. Disapproval of bad habits or behavior is shown by temporarily ignoring someone or by ridiculing them, but this is meant as a way to help the person overcome his problem. It is believed that, ultimately, everyone should be made to feel welcome and important.

HOUSING

In the past, the Lushootseed lived in villages of four or five cedar plank houses, called longhouses. Each longhouse sheltered several related families, and as many as forty people lived in each one. The longhouses measured approximately one hundred feet long and forty feet wide. They were dark and smoky inside, as the doorways were small and there were no windows. A plank in the roof was lifted up to let out smoke from the cooking fires. Fires were kept burning on the dirt floor in front of each family's quarters. From the ceiling hung chunks of smoked salmon, strings of smoked clams, and dried root and herbs.

Along the inside walls were built two wide platforms, one above the other. The people slept on the upper platform and worked on the lower one, which was wider. The space underneath the lower platform was used for storage. The women sewed cattail leaves together for mats, which were hung between each family's section for privacy and warmth. Mattresses and sitting pads were also made of woven cattails.

CLOTHING

Lushootseed clothing was made of cedar bark that had been shredded and pounded. Robes and blankets were made of shredded cedar bark mixed with fireweed fluff and feathers or dog or goat wool, or they were made of bird or animal skins or furs sewn together. Ponchos were made of cattail leaves and hats were made of tightly twined cedar bark.

UTENSILS AND TOOLS

Kitchen utensils were carved out of wood by the men. The women made mats and baskets of grasses, roots, twigs, and other materials gathered during the summer. These materials were soaked and split, cured, and sometimes dyed. They had no metal. Tools were made of horn, bone, or stone, with wooden handles. To cook, women heated stones in a fire and then, using greenwood tongs, placed the stones into tightly coiled cedar root baskets. When the stones cooled, they were replaced with hot ones from the fire.

CANOES

The Lushootseed way of life was based on canoes. Canoes were made of cedar logs, and their size and shape depended on their use. Sharp-ended canoes with high prows were for rough water, as the prows could cut through the water like a wedge. Blunt-ended canoes were for use on rivers and still waters. The canoes were thirty to fifty feet long and could carry twenty to thirty people and their luggage.

Extra curved projections at the bow and stern were carved from separate pieces of cedar and attached to the canoes with pegs and withes of thin cedar limbs. Canoes in use were kept floating in the cove in front of the village. Those not in use were turned over on the beach above the tide line and covered with mats to protect them from the sun.

Sources: *Haboo, Native American Stories of Puget Sound* by Vi Hilbert (University of Washington Press) and *The Eye of the Changer* by Muriel Ringstad (Alaska Northwest Publishing Company)

GLOSSARY

"The Big Lie"—the underlying imaginary premise that students must commit to holding as true when participating in a spontaneous role drama, improvisation, scene, or play

blocking—the planned movement and placement of actors on the stage

casting—choosing who will play which roles in a scene, play, or story dramatization

character—a person, animal, or other being in a story or play with distinguishing physical, vocal, and attitudinal characteristics. The actor's expression of these characteristics is known as "characterization."

choral speaking—a dramatic form in which a text is spoken, in unison or otherwise, by a group of participants

cinquain—a five-line poem, used in this curriculum in the following form:
noun
adjective, adjective
verb, verb, verb
phrase describing the noun
noun

climax—the highest point of tension in a story or play, in which the central conflicts have come to a head but have not yet been resolved

commitment—the strong intent to believe and engage in an imaginary situation; responding to the dramatic situation as if it were real

concentration—the ability to focus and keep one's attention fixed at will to the exclusion of internal or external distractions

context—the thematic framework within which a set of drama activities is presented, including an imaginary situation that motivates and links each of the activities

creative dramatics—"An improvisational, nonexhibitional, process-centered form of theater in which participants are guided by a leader to imagine, enact, and reflect upon human experiences." (As defined by the Children's Theater Association of America.)

Dalcroze Eurhythmics—Named after Emile Jacques Dalcroze (1865–1950), the Swiss musician and educator who developed this approach, Dalcroze Eurhythmics is a method for teaching music through rhythmic movement, ear-training and improvisation

dialogue—words spoken by characters in a story or play, which may be written or improvised

divergent thinking—a form of thinking in which one allows ideas to spread in many directions from a single topic. Divergent thinking often results in unpredictable solutions to problems.

drama —from the Latin for *to do;* encompasses the form, concepts and techniques involved in the expression of thought, feeling, character, and situation through body and voice, action and dialogue. Drama most often portrays or elucidates human experiences.

dramatic form—the form in which traditional works of drama are written, including the elements of exposition, rising action, climax, and resolution

dramatic tension—mental and emotional excitement in drama, born out of a situation of conflict which the audience or participants feel the need to have resolved

dramatization— writing or improvising a story or other piece of literature using elements of dramatic structure including character, action, and dialogue

exposition—the section of a drama, usually at the beginning, that introduces the primary characters and setting and provides the audience with the background information they will need in order to understand the drama's theme and the unfolding of its events

fable—short, traditional story with a moral

fluency—the ability to allow thought or action to flow, unimpeded by constraints

focus—the major point of attention, or the act of directing one's attention. Drama lessons have both an educational focus—the objectives for the lesson, and a dramatic focus—the imaginary situation created to capture and hold the students' attention.

generative art—art that is entirely original, created anew by the artist(s)—as opposed to "interpretive art"

General Space—the space of the entire room in which one is moving. Movement in General Space involves traveling through space.

gesture—an expressive movement of a part of the body that communicates an idea, a feeling, or an attitude

gibberish— dialogue composed of sounds that are not real words. Speaking in gibberish provides students with practice in conveying meaning through their voices rather than relying on words.

imagination—the process of creating a mental picture of something that is not currently present in physical reality

improvisation—the spontaneous creation and performance of action or dialogue in a dramatic form

inner dialogue—the thoughts of an actor as his or her character in a scene or play. The practice of maintaining an inner dialogue keeps actors focused on the action in a scene rather than on how they are appearing to the audience.

in role—assuming a point of view in a role drama; also refers to a technique in drama education in which the teacher or other adult participates in a spontaneous role drama in order to heighten and advance the playing or to manage the students from within the drama

interpretive art—art in which the basic form (words, music, choreography, and so on) has already been created and that is then performed or otherwise interpreted by another artist or artists

kinesphere—the space one's own body takes up, which grows or shrinks depending on how far the limbs are stretched. Your kinesphere travels with you as you move.

Mantle of the Expert—a drama technique in which students work in role as experts with particular knowledge and skills that help them solve an imaginary problem or perform an imagined task. This technique helps students recognize the knowledge they already have while motivating them to expand their learning.

mirroring—a movement activity in which one or more people face a leader and copy his or her movements simultaneously

Movement Story—story narrated by the teacher while students move, the purpose of which is to guide students in developing body awareness and in exploring movement possibilities

pantomime—expressing an idea, feeling, intention, or situation through action without the use of the voice

reflection—thinking about the significance of an event or experience; becoming aware of one's own thoughts, feelings, or values

resolution—the section of a play or drama in which the conflict is resolved. This comes after the climax and is also known as the dénouement.

rising action—the introduction of characters and situations into a play or drama that create complications leading to the climax

ritual—a highly structured, symbolic activity that binds a group to a sense of shared meaning. In drama, use of ritual can encourage commitment to an imaginary situation.

role drama—a drama structure in which a series of events, based on one or more imaginary premises, unfolds spontaneously as participants improvise dialogue or action (see also **spontaneous role drama**)

Self Space—the space directly around one's body. When moving in Self Space, one does not travel.

setting—the physical location of a drama that may be expressed through backdrops, furniture, props, and so forth, or be completely imaginary. Setting sometimes also refers to the entire context of a drama including time period, situation, relationships between characters, and so on.

shadowing—a movement activity in which one or more people follow behind a leader's back and simultaneously imitate his or her movements through space

Sound Story—a story in which the teacher narrates and the students provide appropriate sounds

spectra of theater—the contrasts of Darkness/Light, Sound/Silence, Movement/Stillness, and The Expected/The Unexpected, used to create contrast and tension in a drama

spontaneous role drama—a drama structure in which a series of events, based on one or more imaginary premises, unfolds spontaneously as participants improvise dialogue or action (see also **role drama**)

stance—the position a teacher holds relative to the students when both teacher and student are in role. Some basic stances possible for a teacher in role are: authority (leader, well above the students), facilitator (helper, slightly above the students), member (coparticipant, on the same level as the students) and helpless one (needy, below level of students).

symbol—an object, word or idea used as a focus for thought and feeling, or as a metaphor or representation of a larger idea. In drama, symbols provide a connection between the outer manifestation of a drama and the inner meaning of the experience for the participants.

tableau—a silent, motionless depiction of a scene or image through body position, facial expression, and grouping. Tableaux can be presented with or without props, costumes, or sets.

theater—dramatic performance for an audience that uses action and dialogue to tell a story or otherwise communicate ideas or arouse feelings. The term *theater* can also refer to the building in which such a performance takes place.

upgrade—to raise a drama to a higher level of formality or accuracy, or to deepen its level of significance. The upgrading of a drama may be accomplished through comments by the teacher that encourage reflection or provide accurate technical information, through the teacher's paraphrasing of students' language in a more formal or technically accurate form, or through the use of props that lend an air of professionalism or significance to a scene.

BIBLIOGRAPHY

Books about Child Development and Educational Theory

Ginsburg, Herbert and Sylvia Opper. 1979. *Piaget's Theory of Intellectual Development*. Englewood Cliffs, N.J.: Prentice-Hall, Inc.

Gardner, Howard. 1983. *Frames of Mind*. New York: Basic Books, Inc.

Piaget, Jean and Barbel Inhelder. 1969. *The Psychology of the Child*. New York: Basic Books, Inc.

Books about Drama Education

ArtsConnection. 1995. *"Talent Identification Criteria in Theater Arts,"* Abstract. ArtsConnection.

Bolton, Gavin and Dorothy Heathcote. 1995. *Drama for Learning*. Portsmouth, N.H.: Heinemann.

Dunnington, Hazel Brain and Geraldine Brain Siks editors. 1961. *Children's Theatre and Creative Dramatics*, Seattle, Wash.: University of Washington Press.

Johnstone, Keith. 1979. *Improv*. London: Faber and Faber, Ltd.

McCaslin, Nellie. 1996. *Creative Drama in the Classroom and Beyond*, Sixth Edition. New York: Longman Publishers.

McCaslin, Nellie. 1987. *Creative Drama in the Primary Grades*. New York: Longman, Inc.

Morgan, Norah and Juliana Saxton. 1976. *Teaching Drama*. Great Britain: Stanley Thornes Publishers, Ltd. *(Teaching Drama* must be ordered from England—but it's worth the cost if you are serious about studying role drama.)

Siks, Geraldine Brain. 1958. *Creative Dramatics: An Art for Children*. New York: Harper and Brothers.

Smith, Leisa, Project Director. 1995. *Arts Plus Theatre Curriculum Framework for Elementary Grades K–5*. Helena, Mont.: Helena Presents.

Spolin, Viola. 1986. *Theater Games for the Classroom*. Evanston, Ill.: Northwestern University Press.

Wagner, Betty Jane. 1976. *Dorothy Heathcote / Drama as a Learning Medium*. Washington, D.C.: National Education Association. (*Dorothy Heathcote / Drama as a Learning Medium* can be ordered through the National Education Association.)

Way, Brian. 1967. *Development Through Drama*. Atlantic Highlands, N.J.: Humanities Press.

Wills, Barbara Salisbury. 1996. *Theatre Arts in the Elementary Classroom, Kindergarten Through Grade Three,* Second Edition. New Orleans, La.: Anchorage Press, Inc.

Literature for Dramatization

Fadiman, Clifton. 1984. *The World Treasury of Children's Literature, Books One and Two*. Boston: Little, Brown and Company.

Frey, Charles H. and John W. Griffith editors. 1981. *Classics of Children's Literature*. New York: MacMillan Publishing Company, Inc.

Gerke, Pamela. 1996. *Multicultural Plays for Children Grades K–3* and *Grades 4–6* (two volumes). Lyme, N.H.: Smith and Kraus, Inc.

Gerson, Mary-Joan (retold by). 1992. *Why the Sky is Far Away* (a Nigerian Folktale). Boston: Little, Brown and Company.

Haviland, Virginia (retold by). 1959–1995. *Favorite Fairy Tales Told in*_____ (series). Boston: Little, Brown and Company.

Lattimore, Deborah Nourse. 1987. *The Flame of Peace: A Tale of the Aztecs*. New York: Harper and Row.

McCullough, L.E. 1996. *Plays of America*. Lyme, N.H.: Smith and Kraus, Inc.

Siks, Geraldine Brain. 1964. *Children's Literature for Dramatization*. New York: Harper and Row.

Thistle, Louise. 1998. *Dramatizing Mother Goose*. Lyme, N.H.: Smith and Kraus, Inc.

Turkle, Brinton. 1976. *Deep in the Forest*. New York: The Trumpet Club.

Ward, Winifred. 1952. *Stories to Dramatize*. Anchorage, Ky.: The Children's Theatre.

Winters, Jeanette. 1988. *Follow the Drinking Gourd*. New York: Alfred A. Knopf.

Books about Creative Movement and Dance

Gerke, Pamela and Helen Landalf. 1996. *Movement Stories for Children*. Lyme, N.H.: Smith and Kraus, Inc.

Gilbert, Anne Green. 1992. *Creative Dance for All Ages*. Reston, Va.: American Alliance for Health, Physical Education, Recreation and Dance.

Gilbert, Anne Green. 1977. *Teaching the Three R's Through Movement Experiences*. Minneapolis, Minn.: Burgess Publishing Company.

Landalf, Helen. 1998. *Moving is Relating: Teaching Interpersonal Skills Through Movement in Grades 3–6*. Lyme, N.H.: Smith and Kraus, Inc.

Landalf, Helen. 1997. *Moving the Earth: Teaching Earth Science Through Movement in Grades 3–6*. Lyme, N.H., Smith and Kraus, Inc.

Morningstar, Moira. 1986. *Growing With Dance*. Heriot Bay, B.C.: Windborne Publications.

Books about Lushootseed Salish Culture

Hilbert, Vi. 1985. *Haboo—Native American Stories from Puget Sound*. Seattle: University of Washington Press.

Ringstad, Muriel. *The Eye of the Changer*. Alaska Northwest Publishing Company.

Also Recommended

Smith and Kraus, Inc. "Young Actor's Series" includes many books of monologues, scenes and plays for children. To receive a current catalog call 800-895-4331, or write:

Smith and Kraus, Inc.
PO Box 127
Lyme, N.H. 03768

DISCOGRAPHY

Most of the drama lessons in this book can be presented without music. However, music often motivates self-expression and reduces self-consciousness in children. Several lessons in this book include suggestions for specific musical selections that are listed here, followed by other musical selections that you may find useful for drama and movement activities in general. These have been divided into two general types—active and energetic, and peaceful and relaxing—to help you determine which selections might be suitable for a particular activity.

SELECTIONS SUGGESTED IN THE SECOND-AND THIRD-GRADE DRAMA CURRICULUM LESSONS

Lesson 2:
Chappelle, Eric, "Add on Machine," *Music for Creative Dance: Contrast and Continuum, Volume I*, Ravenna Ventures, Inc. RVCD 9301.

Lesson 16:
Enya, "Caribbean Blue," *Shepherd Moons*, Reprise Records 4-26775.

Mendelssohn, Felix, "Spring Song."

OTHER SELECTIONS FOR DRAMA AND MOVEMENT ACTIVITIES

Active, Energetic
Day Parts, "Morning Blend," *Sunday Morning Coffee*, American Gramaphone Records, AGCD100.

Dead Can Dance, "Bird," *A Passage in Time*, Ryko, RCD 20215.

Penguin Café Orchestra, *Broadcasting From Home* (any selection), Editions EG, EGEDC38.

Roth, Gabrielle and the Mirrors, *Totem* (any selection), Raven Recording, LC5565.

Peaceful, Relaxing

Day Parts, "Across the View," *Sunday Morning Coffee*, American Gramaphone Records, AGCD100.

Nakai, Carlos R., *Earth Spirit* (any selection), Canyon Records, CR-612 Volume 4.

Vollenweider, Andreas, "The Glass Hall," *White Winds*, CBS FMT 39963.

RECOMMENDED COLLECTIONS

- Chappelle, Eric, *Music for Creative Dance: Contrast and Continuum, Volumes I, II, and III,* Ravenna Ventures, Inc., RVCD 9301, 9401 and 9801. These two CDs contain many selections with pauses and alternating phrases; they are excellent for use in exploring movement. Each CD comes with a booklet of Creative Dance teaching ideas.

  To order, call or write:
  Ravenna Ventures, Inc.
  4756 University Village Pl. NE. #117
  Seattle, WA. 98105

- John, Esther "Little Dove," *The Elements, Volumes I and II.* Instrumental music evoking the elements of earth, air, fire, and water.

  To order, write:
  Esther "Little Dove" John and the Mission for Music and Healing
  c/o Church Council of Greater Seattle
  4759 15th Ave. NE.
  Seattle, WA. 98105

- *Classical Cats*, Zanicorn Entertainment, Ltd. ZA01. This is a delightful collection of classical pieces by a variety of composers.

- *One World*, Putamayo World Music, ISBN 1-885265-36-0. This CD is a sampler of music from many cultures, including African, South American, and European. Putamayo World Music also offers other multicultural collections.

ABOUT THE AUTHORS

PAMELA GERKE received her B.A. in English from the University of California at Berkeley and a Multiple Subjects Teaching Credential from Pacific Oaks College in Pasadena, California. She is Artistic Director and Playwright for Kids Action Theater in Seattle, since founding the program in 1988. She has written and/or directed over thirty children's plays. She is also a composer, arranger and conductor for several other shows and for choirs. Pamela is author of *Multicultural Plays for Children, Grades K–6* (in 2 volumes), and *Movement Stories for Children* with Helen Landalf, both published by Smith and Kraus, Inc. She is also the creator of *Doors to Rewards*, a creative reward system for children published by Western Psychological Services. Pamela currently divides her time between Kids Action Theater, arts in education residencies, and composing or arranging music for plays and choirs.

HELEN LANDALF attended the State University of New York at Purchase as a member of the Professional Actor's Training Program, then graduated from the University of Washington in Seattle with a B.A. in Theater Arts and a K–12 Teaching Certification. Helen has performed as both an actress and a dancer, and she currently teaches Creative and Modern Dance for children at the Creative Dance Center in Seattle. She has served as an Artist in Residence for the Montana Public Schools, and she frequently presents workshops for classroom teachers on integrating dance into the basic curriculum. Helen is author of a children's book, *The Secret Night World of Cats*, illustrated by her brother Mark Rimland, *Movement Stories for Children* with Pamela Gerke, *Moving the Earth: Teaching Earth Science Through Movement in Grades 3–6*, and *Moving is Relating: Teaching Interpersonal Skills Through Movement in Grades 3–6*, all published by Smith and Kraus, Inc.